FINDING NICOLE

A True Story of Love, Loss,
Betrayal, Fear and Hope

2.20.21

*Always be the heroine of
your own story!*

♡- Nicole Beverly

For- The Cottage Rabbit

NICOLE BEVERLY

DISCLAIMER

The stories in this book reflect the author's recollection of events. Some names, locations, and identifying characteristics have been changed to protect the privacy of those depicted. Dialogue has been re-created from memory. The Author of this book has utilized police reports obtained through the Freedom of Information Act, Michigan Department of Corrections documents, her own personal safety documentation and court documents in preparing the information in this book.

Some names in the excerpts from police reports have been changed to protect the identities of witnesses. The police report case numbers, dates and all other information noted is directly quoted from each report.

It should be noted that even while I was the victim in these crimes, I had to pay the Michigan State Police over $300 for copies of 3 of my police reports. I also had to pay the Michigan Department of Corrections $398 for copies of my ex-husbands prison records obtained through the Freedom of Information Act simply to prepare for this fight for justice.

This book is dedicated to the hundreds of thousands of victims and survivors of Domestic Violence and Stalking...

No matter who you are and what you have been through, you still matter. Regardless of the physical pain and torture you have been put through, you are still here. Despite the names you have been called and the negative insults that have been hurled at you, you are still enough. No matter how many times you've been told to sit down and be quiet, you still have a voice. You are a survivor.

This book is written in loving memory of the tens of thousands of victims that have been murdered at the hands of their abusers before they could escape or when their pleas for help were ignored by those who had the power to protect them. In their honor I will continue to use my voice to speak our truth until change occurs.

—Nicole Beverly

TABLE OF CONTENTS

BONUS SECTION

NOTE TO READERS

I left my abusive ex-husband eleven years ago in 2009. After leaving my abusive relationship I went on to face years of further abuse at the hands of the legal system that is supposed to protect victims of domestic violence and stalking. Some of the details of my story seem so unbelievable that I would question them myself had I not lived through them. Sadly, my story is not uncommon and many victims of domestic violence and stalking face very similar challenges. I truly consider myself one of the lucky ones because I am still alive despite what I have been through. I am blessed to have a college education and work experience that allow me to support myself and my children. I also have amazing friends and a supportive family who were there to help me when I needed it most. Not every victim is so lucky.

Throughout Finding Nicole I have included excerpts from actual police reports including their identifying report numbers to verify my experiences. Complete police reports are available through the Freedom of Information Act in the State of Michigan for a charge.

In addition to my survival story, I have included a Guidebook Section at the end of this book that I hope will provide both guidance and hope to anyone leaving or recovering from an abusive relationship. The information that I have shared has been collected from other survivors, advocates and experts in the field of Intimate Partner Violence over the past 11 years along my journey from victim to survivor.

In discussing the cover design for this book, my sons asked me to please make sure that the book cover of Finding Nicole was non-descript and looked more like a mystery novel than a domestic violence victim's story and guidebook, so that victims would not be put into further danger if their abusers saw them reading it. This was a very proud moment for me both as a Mother and a Survivor because it told me that my sons truly understand both the dangers and nuances of Domestic Violence. As a result of this conversation, I have placed all the descriptive book information on the inside of Finding Nicole so that it can easily be torn out by the reader if they find it necessary. Another suggestion for readers is to glue an alternative cover onto the front of the book or use a book sleeve if this is an area of concern.

INTRODUCTION

By Angela Dunn, MSW

As a survivor of domestic violence, I joined a few survivors' groups where I was able to connect with and learn from other people who were going through many of the same obstacles. I met Nicole in one of those groups and was immediately drawn to her authenticity, intellect, and determination. I appreciated her transparency about her struggles as a survivor and the respect she showed others. She is also one of the funniest and most quick-witted people I know.

After that first meeting, we quickly became close friends, and through the years I have learned from, been challenged by, and grown because of who Nicole is and the resonate beauty she brings to the world in spite of the terror she has experienced.

The most recent domestic violence statistics show that in the United States nearly 20 people per minute are physically abused by an intimate partner, and more that 20,000 calls are made to domestic violence hotlines each day. *Finding Nicole* offers readers insight into one of those violent cases of abuse.

In this book, Nicole illuminates the myriad, insidious, and often misunderstood ways intimate partners' abuse their victims. But, in her usual and beautiful way, she also highlights many options available to survivors. At the end of this book Nicole includes a "Tips and Tools" section to help readers understand the red flags and warning signs of domestic violence as well as to offer safety tips, recovery tools and a pathway to hope.

I have never met someone with as much tenacity to end domestic violence as Nicole. She has become an expert not only of her lived experience, but also in the field of domestic violence. Her own experiences taught her how to navigate the systems that affect survivors (advocacy, legal, medical, education, etc.), and her dedication to learning ensured her information is relevant for the collective community of survivors. Nicole has helped many survivors and their children start over after they flee from an abuser. She spends countless hours searching for resources for survivors across the country.

Following her passion for prevention efforts, she presents her own curriculum at schools teaching youth about healthy relationships. She has recently started a nonprofit, The ENOUGH Initiative, where she supervises three graduate students, while working full time as a Behavioral Consultant, talks to victims across the country, testifies for legislative initiatives, serves as guest speaker at domestic violence events, and participates in many other activities to help end this epidemic of violence.

Even while Nicole is busy changing the world, she claims her biggest successes can be seen through her sons' resilience and adjustment despite trauma. Through all her trials, her children have been at the forefront of her drive to eradicate domestic violence. They are her purpose, and her home is a safe place full of love and laughter. As a single parent, Nicole continues to bravely lead her family through the trauma to the other side.

Finding Nicole shares intimate details about Nicole's abuse, its effects on her psyche and family. She exposes mind-blowing defects within the legal system that could have cost her family their lives. *Finding Nicole* will take you on a rollercoaster of emotions, make you question everything you take for granted with the justice system, and ignite in you a sense of urgency to join the fight against domestic violence.

Angela Dunn, MSW

FINDING NICOLE

CHAPTER 1

An Unexpected Call

It was April 29th, 2013. I vividly remember sitting at my desk typing up a client's therapy session notes when I got the first of several life altering phone calls that I would receive from law enforcement over course of the next four years.

The detective who called me had a calm tone to his voice, but I could tell that he was struggling with what words to use for whatever he was about to tell me. "Ms. Beverly" he began, "What I am about to tell you may sound frightening", then there was a long pause. "An inmate who is currently housed with your ex-husband at the Washtenaw County Jail has come forward alleging that your ex-husband approached him and offered him $50,000 to kill you."

I held my breath processing the words he had just uttered. Ex-husband, murder, $50,000? I sat quietly waiting for more. The detective went on "The other inmate has passed a polygraph exam and has submitted a written statement about the offer to kill you that he says was made by your ex-husband."

The detective shared that the inmate that had come forward had shared that he was actually considering the offer to kill me but had gotten "cold feet" when he began to think that maybe my ex-husband was trying to set him up for new charges. I quickly realized that what he was saying is that this man had decided to come forward not out of concern for my life but out of concern for his own.

Before ending the phone call the detective added "We are currently still investigating but I wanted to let you know so that you can be aware that other inmates may have been approached with this same offer and haven't come forward." It took me a minute to process his words before I clearly understood what he was trying to tell me. He was saying that other people may have been given this same offer and not come forward and some of them may have already been released. He was subtly telling me that I was at risk for someone else possibly accepting his offer and attempting to kill me.

I was almost afraid to ask my next question, but I needed to know the answer. "How are they planning to kill me?" I asked quietly holding back my tears. The detective responded cautiously, "The plan involves following you either from work or home then sneaking up on you from behind and knocking you out with chloroform then injecting you with a lethal dose of heroine to make it look like an overdose." I was shocked to hear that this was the plan because it would seem so unbelievable to anyone who knows me. I drink occasionally when out with friends, but I don't even smoke cigarettes let alone inject heroine.

"So, what happens next?" I asked quietly. "Will there be new charges against him for attempting to hire someone for murder?" I didn't even know if that was the correct term to use but it was the only thing that came to mind from the movies and crime TV shows that I had watched. The detective explained to me that the case was now in the Washtenaw County Prosecutor's hands and that it would be up to them to decide if they would be moving forward with new charges. He stated that he or someone from the Prosecutor's office would be contacting me with an update.

Over the next few days, the reality of what I had been told began to sink in more and I sat with feelings of fear, anxiety and oddly enough at the same time hope. Hope that there would be new charges against my ex-husband, and that he would get another, longer prison sentence that would keep me and my two sons safe longer. Fear and anxiety because now I knew that there was the possibility of other people out there willing to take him up on his offer to kill me while he was still behind bars thinking that would give him the perfect alibi.

Excerpts from actual police report

CR #120054153 Date: 04/29/2013

On 4/27/13 I received an email from Desk Sergeant Kline that Washtenaw County inmate Jerry Smith had relayed information to a corrections officer that he had been approached by fellow inmate Kevin Beverly. Beverly had reportedly asked Smith if he would be willing to kill his wife when he got out of prison.

Smith advised that approximately four days ago he and Beverly were outside of their cells and began having a conversation about their respective cases, and about what prison was like (as Smith had previously spent time in prison and Beverly had not). Smith advised that Beverly was speaking about his own case and more specifically his ex-wife. Beverly advised, "That bitch put me in prison, I'd like to get rid of that bitch. I'd pay $50,000 to put her in the ground." Smith replied, "How much would you pay upfront?" Beverly advised that he would, "Pay up to $50,000, I have a nice life insurance policy on her." Smith replied that he would be interested but would have to see the policy prior to any agreement.

The conversation continued, and Beverly advised that they could meet somewhere once they had both been released, and that he would show him the policy at that time. Beverly advised that he had thought about a plan for the murder, and that that if his ex-wife was car-jacked then pistol whipped or shot up with a lethal dose of heroin, it would look like an accidental overdose. They agreed that they could meet at a location in Canton which is in another County, as Beverly assumed that he would likely be on a GPS tether upon his release.

They also exchanged MDOC numbers so that they could keep track of one another. Smith added that he was hoping for a "temporary insanity" plea that would allow him to be released sooner, while Beverly hoped that he would get to go to Bootcamp. They also agreed to stay in touch via letter and "minute phones" which would be difficult to trace.

Smith advised that there was another conversation that occurred on 4/28/13 while he and Beverly were outside "in the yard". Smith was walking laps when he was again approached by Beverly. The conversation quickly turned to the murder plot. Smith advised that he would need $500-$1000 dollars upfront, and would then expect the remainder to be paid after Beverly's ex-wife had been killed. Beverly agreed to this. He advised that his ex-wife lived in Ypsilanti with their two children. He told Smith not to do anything in front of the children. He also provided his ex-wife's work location. Smith advised that he would like to use Chloroform to knock out Beverly's ex-wife, then shoot her up with a lethal does of heroin. Beverly asked why he wouldn't simply knock her out, and Smith replied that there would likely be a mark left behind that could be discovered at autopsy. When the conversation ended and they returned inside it occurred to Smith that Beverly may be setting him up. As a result he approached a corrections officer on his block and told him about the conversations he and Beverly had been having. This was apparently how this situation came to light. Smith stated that any further cooperation on his behalf would require some degree of consideration of leniency in his own robbery cases.

Further actions: I advised Smith that he would have to submit to, and pass, a polygraph examination regarding his statements. Smith readily agreed to this. I advised him that he would have to stand by while I made arrangements for a polygraph. Smith advised that he was ready to take the test but added that he would like to return to his cell while he waited so that other inmates would not become suspicious. I then escorted Smith back to the WCJ with the understanding that I would return for him later that afternoon when the polygraph examiner had arrived.]

[Polygraph examination: Later that same day polygraph examiner Howard Ross arrived in the Detective Bureau. I briefed Ross on the case, then retrieved Smith from the jail. I turned him over for the examination. Later that afternoon I met with Ross who advised that Smith had been found to be truthful in his statement to me. I told Smith that he had passed the examination, and that I would be returning him to the jail. I advised that I would be re-contacting him as soon as I had an opportunity to speak to someone from the Washtenaw County Prosecutor's Office. Please refer to the attached copy of the polygraph examination report for specific information.]

Further actions: I contacted Assistant Prosecutor Slawson with the information regarding statement and polygraph results. Slawson advised that she would meet with her supervisors to discuss any possibility of moving forward and providing the potential of providing any consideration towards Smith and his pending cases.

Detective Mark Babbs #5515

CHAPTER 2

Growing Up Nicole

I arrived in this world November 21, 1972 in Pontiac, Michigan weighing in at 10 lbs 6 ounces. I was born into a family that was caring, hardworking and financially secure. My immediate and extended family members were mostly Caucasian of various cultural descents and backgrounds.

My mother, Sally already had her bachelor's degree in education when I was born and taught Second Grade for many years for the Pontiac School District before she went back to school to complete her master's degree in Reading Intervention when I was in high school.

My father was a test driver for Ford Motor Company when I was born then later was able to get back to the field he was passionate about when he became a staff photographer, then head of photography at The Ford Motor Company Test Track in Romeo, Michigan where he worked until he retired.

I only have one sibling, a sister, Christine, who is 10 years older than me. Because of our age difference by the time I was in second grade she was already heading off to college. My paternal Grandmother Jane passed away from breast cancer when I was four years old, so my Grandfather Joe Sr. moved in with us and was a major caregiver in my life for as long as I can remember.

My maternal grandparents, Bernice and Orrin Huntoon lived in Pontiac at one of the family's Funeral Home's that they had owned and operated for generations.

When I was four years old my family moved to Lapeer, Michigan. A small, rural, mostly Caucasian town with dirt roads, corn fields for miles and a one screen movie theater. My house sat on 10 acres of land and the closest neighbors were at least a 6-minute walk by road or a 3-minute run cutting through the woods or fields.

We weren't a religious family but my parents talked to me about religion and spirituality and taught me that God or whatever higher powers there may be cared more about how you treated other people and helped others than how often you went to church. My parents always encouraged me to research and explore different religions rather than telling me what religion I had to follow.

In hindsight I always felt a little different than most of the other kids growing up in that very small and very "white" farm town. I spent my childhood listening to Bob Marley, Steel Pulse, Eek a Mouse, Blues, Jazz, & lots of Bob Dylan, Neil Young and Van Morrison.

My Dad would read Beatnik authors like Jack Kerouac, Allen Ginsberg and William Burroughs aloud to us from a very young age while most parents were probably reading Goodnight Moon and Little Red Riding Hood. If you aren't familiar with the Beatniks they often wrote about their open disdain for cultural norms, the exploration of Eastern Religions like Buddhism as well as Native American spirituality and sexual liberation.

One thing however that my parents never taught me about or prepared me for was that there were people in this world who were cruel, manipulative and abusive. Like most parents they probably never felt the need to have this conversation with me or thought that I needed to know the red flags of these abusive individuals to avoid getting involved in a relationship with one of them.

My mother has always been a very strong woman and she taught me that my gender should never be a barrier that keeps me from doing or accomplishing anything that I want to. I remember her telling me at a young age that I wouldn't be a cheerleader because girls play sports, they don't just stand around cheering for boys that do.

Fortunately, I had no desire to be a cheerleader because I was way too clumsy so her stance on that never bothered me. Tennis, basketball and softball were more my speed. I would have to say that I was what people would call a "Tomboy" growing up. My two closest neighbors and best friends were boys, Daniel and Scott and together we spent hours exploring the woods, playing baseball, football, ditch diving and rope swinging in Scott's cow barn.

My mom taught in an urban school district and I would often spend time at her school when my school had breaks. My entire life my parents had a diverse group of friends whose families we would often spend time with. The older that I got the more I realized how incredibly segregated the town we lived in was. Because I had been raised differently than many of my peers who weren't taught to embrace different cultures and religions I remember getting into arguments when peers at school would say racist or other insensitive things.

There were times I would come home so upset that my mother would file complaints with my high school principal. I thought she might lose her mind the day that I came home and told her about our senior year "Slave Auction" fundraiser and the times I would share the blatantly racist comments made by my biology teacher.

I am quite sure that my mother's willingness to always stand up for what was right was a large part of the reason that I too grew up to be very outspoken and assertive in my beliefs.

In high school I always danced to my own beat but joined in with lots of other drummers... I had friends in pretty much every "stereotypical group" there was back in the late 80's from "the jocks" to "Heathers or mean girls" to "the nerds" to "the stoners". I was always able to bounce back and forth between them without missing a beat.

I had a serious boyfriend, Jeff throughout my junior and senior years of high school and we were so happy and in love that I was sure I was going to marry him. We would talk about someday having our own house after we graduated from college, got great jobs and that we would of course have three beautiful children, 2 dogs and a cat. That plan didn't work out the way we imagined after we went to different colleges after high school and quickly grew apart from one another.

My parents rarely fought in front of me growing up that I can remember. Looking back now I can see that my Dad has always had difficulty sharing his feelings and if he was upset about something, he would kind of just disappear to do yard work, take care of our growing collection of animals or go running. My Mom was the more active and at times overly controlling parent in our house.

Both of my parents were runners, and, in many ways, I think they used that as an escape from one another as their relationship began to deteriorate. There was never yelling, screaming or violence in our house instead there was silence... at times to the point of discomfort. By the time I was in high school it became obvious that neither of them was happy in the relationship and that silence would often extend to me.

My sister who was ten years older than me was already married and had started her own family. Looking back now I remember that I often felt alone and isolated when I was at home because they were clearly both unhappy and trying to find their own way. I have very few memories of what a healthy relationship should look and feel like. They eventually divorced after my freshman year of college after 35 years of marriage.

CHAPTER 3

A New Sense of Fear

On May 4th, 2013 I received the return phone call that I had anxiously been waiting for from the detective who had notified me about my ex-husband's attempt to hire someone to kill me from jail.

The detective let me know that the inmate who had come forward was now requesting a deal that involved taking time off his sentence in exchange for his testimony. He added that the prosecutor's office was refusing to bargain with him which meant no new charges would be issued against my ex-husband.

He went on to say that he had spoken to the warden at the prison my ex-husband would be transferred to and that they would "keep an eye on him in prison" and that "his prison file would be marked with an alert that this attempt to hire had occurred so they would be watchful for future attempts to hire." I was still naïve enough at this point to believe that this was true.

After that conversation I was equal parts devastated, angry and afraid. I had believed that now that my ex-husband was finally incarcerated after years of stalking and threatening to kill me that I would finally have peace. That I would have some time to live my life without constant fear, having to look over my shoulder and triple checking locks.

Instead I now knew that I didn't have just him to fear. I was also in danger of someone else, a stranger who might be willing to take him up on his offer of $50,000 and may try to kill me. A stranger who could approach me at any time, any place and without any warning attempt to harm me.

I was stunned that this was it, no further investigation, no more negotiation with the inmate that had come forward, case closed. I was also in shock that he again had no consequences for his actions and was continuing to instill fear in me even from prison.

Excerpt from Police Report #120054153-015

CR No: 120054153-015 Date 05/06/2013

On 4/30/13 I received a phone call from Assistant Prosecutor Slawson advising that she had spoken to her supervisors and they had determined that due to the severity and recidivistic nature of Smith's cases they would not be willing to make him any offers whatsoever.

On 5/5/13 I received an "Inmate Communication Kite" from Smith asking that I contact him regarding this situation. At that time, I went to the WCJ and found that Smith was outside in the yard with the rest of the inmates from his block. I advised Corrections Officer West, who was supervising Smith's block at that time, of the decision that had been made by the prosecuting attorney's office. I asked Officer West to discreetly relay this information to Smith.

On 5/6/13 I also met with Commanders Helen and Worth, as well as Lieutenants Kline and Green regarding this situation. At that time I was directed to contact the MDOC staff at the Egeler Reception Center to notify them of the situation regarding Kevin Beverly. Beverly had been transported to Egeler earlier that morning.

Later that same day I contacted the Deputy Warden at the Egeler Reception Center. I verified that Beverly had arrived at the facility. I briefed the warden on Beverly's attempts to arrange a "murder for hire" plot against his ex-wife. The warden advised that she would note this in her file and also specify that Beverly and Smith would never be housed together at any time. The warden also advised me that she would re-contact me should an future relevant information became available regarding either of these individuals.]

Disposition: Informational report only

Status: Closed

Detective Mark Babbs #5515

CHAPTER 4

Growing Up Kevin

My ex-husband's childhood was much different than mine. He too was born in November of 1972 ironically at the same hospital as me in Pontiac, Michigan. Kevin was born into an African American family that lived in an urban neighborhood for several years before being one of the first black families to move to the suburb of Southfield, Michigan. He had one brother who was four years older.

His biological mother, who was a teacher left his father when Kevin was two years old. On numerous occasions she explained to me that she left the relationship due to physical and emotional abuse by Kevin's father who was a school principal by that time. She also shared that when the boys were 4 and 8 the custody battle and threats made by Kevin's father became extreme and she made the decision to move to Missouri to live with her Mother without the boys.

This was a decision that significantly impacted Kevin and resulted in feelings of anger and resentment towards his biological mother. He would talk about it often stating that he could not understand how any Mother could just leave her children that way.

Kevin's father remarried when Kevin was 3 years old and his new wife, a physician brought two children of her own into the family, a daughter who was 4 years older than Kevin and a son who was 6 years older. Shortly after they were married, his father and stepmother had another daughter together.

From Kevin's reports his childhood was filled with both good and negative memories. He shared that his father was always very strict and was never a warm or loving person. He told me that he remembered several incidents of his dad being both emotionally and physically abusive towards his stepmother and his older biological brother.

By the time I met his family his dad and stepmom were still married but had been living separately for several years, however they would come together for holidays and family events. I remember thinking it was strange, but it was explained to me that for them to be able to further their careers they both had to move to different locations that were far apart and made it too difficult for them to commute. During these periods of family separation Kevin always resided with his dad.

CHAPTER 5

Leaving Lapeer

During my Senior year of high school I was accepted to a few of the in state colleges that I had applied to and ultimately decided to attend Eastern Michigan University because they had a good Social Work program and it was near the city of Ann Arbor and the University of Michigan so I knew it would provide me with new experiences and lots of things to do outside of classes.

My freshman year of college was a year of exploring my newfound freedom without my Mom watching my every move. I drank too much, partied too hard and studied way too little but somehow managed to pass all but one of my classes that year. I made new friendships and was happy to be living in a town where diversity was not just normal but embraced.

After my high school relationship had broken up pretty early in my Freshman year, I started dating a senior on the basketball team only to find out that my new "superstar" boyfriend was also still dating his high school girlfriend and had apparently forgotten to mention that to me. After that experience I became more guarded with whom I trusted and gave my time to. Or at least so I thought.

CHAPTER 6

The Perfect Victim

I met my now ex-husband, Kevin in 1991 when we were both just 18 years old and beginning our Sophomore year at Eastern Michigan University. I had seen him around campus the year before and we had mutual friends. I also would see him on my dorm floor occasionally as he had been dating someone that lived down the hall from me.

As I was beginning my Sophomore year of college, I was excited about school and returning to see my friends. I remember that I was still feeling a little sad and hurt that my high school boyfriend had moved on to a new girlfriend and really had no interest in rekindling our relationship while we were both home over the summer.

One evening shortly after school had started, I ran into my now ex-husband Kevin while we were both returning to our dorms after classes. He stopped and introduced himself to me and we spoke for a while about our summers and school restarting. He was pleasant and funny. Kevin shared that he was glad to be back at school but was really busy with classes and practice as he was the center on our college football team.

As we walked back, I discovered that Kevin lived in the athletic dorm that was directly across the street from mine. We said our goodbyes and I went back to my dorm.

One evening a few weeks later while I was sitting out on the front steps of my dorm waiting for my friend to return, I heard someone calling my name from across the street. It was Kevin and he was yelling to me from his dorm window. He told me to come over and say hello. I had been waiting quite a while for my friend who was notoriously late so I decided that I may as well go say "Hi".

Once I got to his dorm room and he introduced me to his roommates he offered me a beer which I gladly accepted. We sat and drank beer and talked for what turned out to be hours and I completely forgot about the friend that I had been waiting for earlier that night. He was cute, funny, charming and intelligent. We talked about all sorts of things and realized that we had a lot of similar interests and enjoyed spending time together.

After that first night we started spending time together often. If we weren't in classes or he wasn't at practice, we were together. I began staying the night in his dorm often because his roommate was staying at his girlfriend's most nights. Things were really going well. We had fun together, we talked about deep topics, we were silly with each other and the chemistry between us was undeniable.

One of my closest friends my Freshman year was on the men's basketball team and we had stayed in touch over the summer and he would occasionally stop by my dorm to hang out or we would go out and do things together. Fairly early on in our relationship Kevin told me that he was not okay with that friendship and did not want me hanging out with him anymore.

I remember trying to explain that it was nothing more than a friendship but eventually telling him that I understood why that would bother him and I agreed to stop spending time with that friend.

For the next few months other than a few negative comments about my friends or questions about my whereabouts, things were still going great. We were growing closer and falling in love. He would tell me painful things about his parents and his childhood that he said he had never told anyone before.

He would tell me that he loved and trusted me more than anyone he had ever met before. I continued to spend most of my free time with him at his dorm room and began to do less and less with my friends who expressed their annoyance with me. I just took it as them being jealous that I was happy and had found someone that I was in love with.

I would go to his football games and cheer him on. He was playing well and was named as one of the team Captains by his head coach. Everything was good, we had each other and nothing else mattered.

Looking back now I can see how things began to change even during that first year. There were days that he would be very short and curt with me that I explained away as him just being tired. He began putting down my friends and saying negative things about them whenever I made plans with them. I explained it away as he just wanted me spending time with him because he loved me so much.

Then there were the nights that I wouldn't hear from him and he would tell me that he had "fallen asleep at another football players house" or was too drunk after a party to drive home. I explained that away by telling myself that he loved me and was telling the truth because he had no reason to lie.

We continued to date throughout our Junior and Senior years of college. Again, in hindsight I can see so many things that I did not know were red flags occurring during those two years. He isolated me even further from my friends by telling me how much he disliked them and how they were negative influences on me.

When we argued everything began to become my fault and he was very good at twisting and turning circumstances to make me consider or even believe that his point of view might be the truth. I started to change my behavior and be less myself to not upset him and to avoid arguments.

Kevin also began to put me down if we were arguing or he didn't like something I had done or said. I remember being so hurt when he would call me stupid" or a "fat ass". He would of course apologize and tell me that he didn't really mean it and would be extra sweet for several days afterwards.

The more that happened the more put down's and name calling happened the more I began to question if these things were true about me and my self-esteem began to take hit regardless if he apologized afterwards or not.

I was also beginning to hear rumors about him seeing other girls and cheating on me which he would of course deny. Any time I tried to talk to him about that or anything else that wasn't a topic he wanted to discuss, I became a "nag" or an "annoying bitch" and he would ask if he was supposed to not want to cheat if his girl was always on him about something.

Again, I began to question myself and if I was really being unreasonable or annoying. Most of my friends could not stand him by this point and would try to talk to me about their concerns, but I was so in love I didn't want to hear it.

In hindsight I can see how much I changed over the course of those three years. It was that early on when I began to doubt myself, believe him when he said that I was the cause of most of our problems and I began to feel like I wasn't good enough.

I began to believe that I wasn't smart enough, thin enough, pretty enough, passive enough, etc. That I didn't deserve the relationship that we had in the beginning that felt so amazing and perfect.

I was the perfect victim because while I was a strong young woman, I was also an empathic young woman who wanted to help, understand and fix people who were hurting. I was going to school for social work and learning about how early childhood experiences could impact someone's life.

I wanted to help Kevin, I loved him and even though he at times made me feel horrible about myself he would eventually always apologize and promise to change. I bought it time and time again because I wanted us to go back to the way things were in the beginning. In my mind if things had been that good, they could go back to being that good again.

CHAPTER 7

Betrayal

Kevin and I dated on and off for the next 9 years before we finally decided to get married. He ended up playing both Canadian and Arena Football for a few years after college and would be out of the State for extended periods of time so we would "take breaks". There would also be times when things just got too bad because he was so mean and cold to me or it was so obvious that he was cheating on me that I would finally get the strength to break up with him.

Eventually though he always made his way back into my life with the perfect words, apologies and promises to change.

In 1999 our son Myles was unexpectedly conceived while I was taking double antibiotics for a sinus infection and acne treatment. While things were far from perfect at that time we were doing okay. We both had good jobs, I was a Social Worker for the State of Michigan and he was an Ann Arbor Police Officer.

I had purchased my first little 900 sq ft house in Ann Arbor just down the street from my job during one of our break ups and it just made sense that Kevin would move in before our son was born.

Once Myles was about 6 months old, we decided that now that we had a child together, we were committed to each other even more and that we should purchase a larger home together since mine was so small. I listed my house and within a few months we had some great offers. We began looking at homes and put an offer on one that seemed perfect for a new family.

Within days of me selling my current home and our offer being accepted on the house we intended to buy, Kevin announced to me that he had changed his mind and no longer wanted to buy a home together. At first, I thought that he had to be joking because I could not believe what he was telling me.

I had never in my life felt so betrayed by someone... Nothing had happened to make him change his mind, no argument, no huge fight. He refused to have an in-depth conversation with me about it and would simply tell me that he just wasn't ready to commit to me at that level. I was beside myself... I was already overwhelmed as I was a first-time mother with a new baby, was in graduate school, working and now would have nowhere to live.

Because I had already committed to selling my home and being out within the next 60 days there was nothing I could do but figure out where I was going to go with my infant child. At that point I had already started Graduate School at Eastern Michigan University as well, so location was important in deciding what I was going to do.

I was incredibly devastated and embarrassed because my family and friends knew that I had sold my home and that we had plans to move together into a new larger home for our family. Embarrassed that he cared so little that he could just bail on me, on us at the last minute. To make matters even worse Kevin refused to move out stating that he needed time to figure out where he was going to move first.

Those 60 days felt like a lifetime. Having to see him every day and know that he was the person ripping my life apart after he had promised to change made me feel absolutely sick and heartbroken.

I finally reached out to my parents because I had no idea what to do and they suggested that I move home with them until I could figure out what made the most sense for me to do.

At that point in time I had two dogs, Emo, and Italian Greyhound and Dino, an energetic Pitbull mix and I loved them both dearly. Since I was going to be moving in with my parents with a baby there was not going to be room for two dogs. I was devastated and begged Kevin to take Dino with him until I could get my own place and move him in with me and he surprisingly agreed.

CHAPTER 8

Hanging on by a Thread

Just A few weeks after we both moved and I was settled into my parents' house over an hour away in Shelby Township and Kevin had moved into his new apartment still in the Ann Arbor area, he decided that he wanted to begin spending time with our son.

He threatened to go court and fight for shared custody if I didn't comply. I reluctantly agreed to one overnight visit every other weekend and even after we agreed to that he of course would cancel on a regular basis.

Approximately a month after we both moved, I called Kevin to see if he needed anything for Dino that I could bring the next time I brought Myles out to see him. He casually informed me that he had decided to take my dog to the Humane Society and surrender him because he was "too much work".

He had not called me, give me a chance to rehome him or even discuss it with me before dropping my dog off at the shelter. I was heartbroken. I had had that dog for the past four years and had nursed him back to life from the parvovirus. I didn't think it was possible for me to feel any worse than I already did but Kevin continued to prove me wrong.

There were moments that I was so depressed, I thought of ways that I could take my own life and make it look like an accident. Knowing that I now had a beautiful baby who I loved dearly and needed me, I knew I couldn't to give in to those thoughts of an easy escape from my feelings of sadness and hopelessness.

I recognized that I was having feelings of depression that were unhealthy and I began to see a counselor and take an antidepressant to hopefully help improve my mood and make me feel more like myself again.

The longer I was away from Kevin the better I felt. I had started taking walks and spending more time with my friends from graduate school, working on projects and commuting to and from school together.

I became close with one person in particular, James, who coincidentally had played college football with Kevin but who I really never knew while we were in college as he was a year older and didn't really hang out with the same circle of friends that Kevin and I did.

It was James who helped me paint and put the border up in Myles new room at my parents' house, he would help me with Myles while we were working on school projects and he always made me laugh and treated me with kindness knowing everything that I was going through.

He was there when Myles said his first words and took his first steps. He was there when Myles was sick, when I was struggling, or when I needed help getting through a graduate project.

Over the next few months, we became closer and eventually it became obvious that we had feelings for each other which is the absolute last thing that I expected or even wanted at that time. We talked about it and the fact that I was part of a package deal with an infant child and he laughed that I felt the need to even bring that up considering the fact that he had been the one helping me take care of that infant child for most of the past 6 months.

Because I had been betrayed by Kevin so many times over the past 9 years, I did not trust anyone or anything. I continued to spend time with James and my feelings for him grew over time. Those feelings were real and deep, but I was terrified to get hurt again so I always kept a wall up to a certain degree.

By now it had been almost a year since I had moved in with my parents and I was feeling more and more like myself again. I think Kevin began to realize this and he began to realize that I was okay with being on my own even with an infant child.

That is when the calls from Kevin started again about how he realized now what a huge mistake he had made and how he wanted to be a full-time father to his son.

He had gotten a job as a pharmaceutical sales representative a few months earlier and was making much better money that he was as a police officer, so he said that he was feeling much more financially secure and was ready to become a family again.

I told him multiple times that I was not interested and did not even want to talk to him about anything but the custody exchanges of our child.

Kevin of course became even more persistent and began driving to my parents' home to pick up our son and to do things like go trick or treating or take him to the park. He always used these moments as an opportunity to try and talk me into coming back and being a family again.

He would tell me how much better off our son would be if he had two parents and a father who was involved. He even went as far as buying me a $7,000 engagement ring and proposing to me multiple times despite my refusals.

At some point during this time Kevin became very suspicious about my relationship with James and began asking me more and more questions about him and our friendship.

This went on for months and one evening Kevin drove by and saw James's car at my parents' house which sent him through the roof.

From that point forward his efforts to get me back went back and forth between declaring his love for me and begging me to come back and threatening to hurt James if he didn't leave me alone.

I remember feeling so torn and confused because I had feelings for James, I loved him, and I did not want anything bad to happen to him because of me. I also remember thinking it would just be easier if I went back so Kevin would just stop the dramatics and that maybe he was right when he said that it would be better to be a family again.

I remember hoping that maybe he had changed this time... I mean he had gone so far as to buy me an engagement ring and was buying a condo closer to my parents in Sterling Heights because he said he knew it would be easier for me if he was living closer by.

CHAPTER 9

Intuition

Looking back now it is difficult for me to remember the exact reasons that I ultimately decided to go back with Kevin at that point. I think it was a combination of fear, frustration and a very small amount of hope.

Kevin had escalated his threats about harming James and had even gone so far as to start calling him at his job, telling him that he knew where his office was and would be waiting for him to leave work. I felt so guilty and responsible for this amazing man that I had come to love having to worry about his safety because of me that it absolutely broke my heart.

It felt so unfair to put him in this position and looking back I know that at that point in time I truly did not believe that I was worth someone else being put through something like this because of me... That I was not worthy of real love and someone who truly cared about me and was willing to stand by me through this difficult time.

I let James know what I was feeling, and I can only imagine that he was probably relieved, frustrated and angry all at the same time. Not angry with me but angry at the situation and what Kevin was doing to both of us.

When I told Kevin that I would come back I let him know firmly that if we were not married within 6 months or if he began treating me poorly again, I was leaving and would never give this relationship another chance. Deep down inside I thought that was my going to be my out because I never thought that he would go through with getting married or make it 6 months whole months without going back to his old ways.

On November 21, 2001 the two of us drove to Toledo, Ohio without telling anyone and got married at the courthouse. During the entire ride there my intuition was telling me not to go through with this. Even if he had made it 6 months without a major incident and that things felt okay on the surface my gut was yelling at me not to go through with the marriage.

Somehow, I pushed those internal voices that were screaming at me to stop and not go through with this out of my head and I went ahead with the very bland and uneventful marriage ceremony.

CHAPTER 10

Things Begin to Escalate

After getting married things continued to be mostly good for a while. We welcomed our second son, Carter into the world in September 2003 and in October 2003 moved into our beautiful new home in Ypsilanti, Twp.

We had picked out everything for our new home from the ground up and I was feeling excited and happy for the first time in a very long while.

From 2004 until 2008 things would follow a typical pattern of emotional abuse. Things would be good for a while, then tension would build, he'd have an escalation of emotion and would lash out at me with mean words, name calling and blaming me for everything wrong in the relationship. This emotional escalation would then be followed with apologies, excuses, promises to change and gifts or kind gestures.

At this point in time I still was not fully aware that I was in an abusive relationship. From the outside looking in things looked great and we were the perfect family with two beautiful children, a beautiful home, nice cars and devoted parents. I had no idea what emotional abuse really looked like or that I was in an abusive relationship myself.

In 2008 something began to quickly change, and things began to escalate. Kevin went from just name calling and blame to throwing things at me, gesturing as if he was going to hit me and making threatening statements along with the name calling. The apologies and promises to change became less genuine and more infrequent.

I remember getting Myles. ready for bed one night and him asking me "why I stayed with daddy?" I asked him what he meant, and he said, "because he is so mean to you." I held back my tears and made up some excuse about his job being stressful and walked straight to my bathroom where I shut my door and burst into tears.

It was at that moment that I realized I wasn't doing as good of a job as I thought I was hiding how bad the relationship had become. My children were being affected a lot more than I realized by their Dad's behavior towards me. My beautiful home was becoming a place that I didn't even want to be... it was becoming my prison.

CHAPTER 11

The Birds Nest

By June of 2009 the incidents of verbal abuse by my then husband were growing both in frequency and intensity. He was drinking more than ever and blaming the stressors of his sales job for him needing to drink more to help him "relax".

We were both working full time, taking care of the boys, the household duties, daycare pickups and after school sports.

Because of his sales calls he was rarely available to help with anything at the house or for our children so most of the family duties were falling on me alone.

It seemed like he was always angry about something no matter how minor and everything that he was angry about seemed to be my fault again.

Kevin would become upset and start calling me repeatedly if he felt that I was at the grocery store for too long or spent too much time on play dates for the boys at friend's houses. He would tell me that I was "taking too fucking long." and that I needed to "get my fat ass home!"

He was regularly calling me a "stupid bitch" and telling me how lazy, fat, ugly and stupid I was. He often felt the need to tell me that my opinion didn't matter and that I should just "shut my fat fucking mouth".

Kevin seemed to most love telling me how no one else would ever want to be with me and that I would never find someone that really loved me. He told me this often and I had begun to believe it.

At the same time the emotional warfare was increasing, he was also becoming more and more physically abusive towards me. Things like twisting my arm behind my back, pushing me down, grabbing my face, bumping into me, raising a fist or slapping me on the head with his fist or objects were happening on a regular basis where in the past they only happened occasionally.

I had not told anyone what was happening behind closed doors because I was still confused about what to do, afraid of him and embarrassed that I was tolerating his behavior.

I began to make excuses for the bruises and marks that were visible if someone asked. I became very good at lying to friends and coworkers and pretending that everything was fine at home or quickly changing the subject. I was truly struggling with what I should do and if I should leave the marriage and if I did how to do so safely.

I remember being so unhappy and miserable with our relationship that I looked forward to going to work every day as it had become my only safe place to be for 8 hours a day.

One warm evening in June we took the boys out to dinner where he was drinking excessively which wasn't out of the ordinary anymore. When we returned home, we immediately noticed that our front porch and foyer window were splattered with bird poop from the birds that built a next on the top ledge of our foyer window.

As we exited the car Kevin became visibly upset and proceeded to get the garden hose and spray down the nest along with the baby birds that were inside of it.

My sons were excited to see the baby birds at first but quickly realized that my ex-husband intended on killing them and they both became upset, especially my younger son Carter who loved animals so much.

I begged for him to stop and not kill the baby birds in front of the boys, but he continued to do so despite my pleas. I decided that the best thing to do in the moment was to take my children to my mother's house for a few hours until they were calm, and he was less agitated.

I went into the house to get my car keys and told the boys to get into my vehicle. My ex-husband came into the garage and began screaming at them to get into "the fucking house" and go up to their rooms. They were both crying and afraid, but they knew better than to not follow his orders.

I could tell that something was different about his level of anger that night. When I saw the contempt in his eyes and the way that he was looking at me as he told me that I would never take his children away from him, I knew I wasn't safe and attempted to run out of the garage.

As I ran towards the door, he caught my ponytail from behind and dragged me back towards the house. I screamed for help as he dragged me backwards into the house praying that one of my neighbors had heard me and would call 911.

Once he got me into the laundry room just inside of the house, he shut the garage door and proceeded to violently attack me. He kicked, choked, punched and slapped me with his fists and shoes that we stored in the laundry room. He pressed his full weight into my rib cage until I heard a crack. He repeatedly told me to "shut my fucking mouth" and to "stop crying like a little bitch before he gave me even more to cry about."

I remember the look in his eyes was terrifying that night. They somehow looked both vacant and menacing at the same time. I can't remember if I lost consciousness or not that night, but I do remember seeing stars and floating lines as he choked me and repeatedly struck me in the head.

At some point during the attack he made the decision to drag me into the kitchen and ordered me to sit at the kitchen table while he went into his office that was in the next room.

He took my keys, my cell phone and the house phone with him. He ordered me not to move a muscle and told me that he would kill me if I did. I remember sitting at the kitchen table trying to figure out if I had enough time to run out the door without him catching me or shooting me from behind as I ran. I was praying that my boys wouldn't come downstairs because I knew there was nothing, I could do at that point to protect them.

After what felt like only seconds he returned with his handgun and ordered me to kneel before him on the floor. He told me that I better pray that no one heard my pleas for help and called the police because if they did and the cops showed up at our door, he planned to shoot them when he opened the door before he killed me.

I don't remember how long I kneeled on that living room floor, but it felt like hours. I was sure that he was going to kill me, and I remember thinking about my boys and how they would ever get over this happening to them. I also remember telling myself that I should have left him while I still had the chance.

I remember his saying "pray bitch.", as he held the gun to my head. He continued to hold the gun to my head as he told me all of the things that he thought were wrong with me and all the reasons that he should kill me.

He told me that "I was a horrible mother, I was a bad wife, I was fat and ugly, I didn't deserve him, I was lazy and a stupid bitch, etc...". Every few minutes he would pull the gun away from my head and unload the clip then put it back in and back to my head like it was a game. I could tell that he was getting enjoyment from the power he had over me and seeing me in so much pain and fear.

I can't explain why he didn't pull the trigger that night because I was certain that he would and that would be the last day I would ever see my children. My pleas for him to stop just aggravated him more and he would scream at me to "stop crying and shut your fucking mouth." I was prepared for him to pull that trigger at any moment and accepted that death was inevitable so I stopped responding unless it was to admit to something he was accusing me of or some character flaw that he said that I had.

At some point during that night, he must have gotten tired of the game he was playing and apparently decided not to pull the trigger. He forced me to go upstairs and sleep next to him. He had locked my keys and phones in his office so that I couldn't access them. I of course was not able to fall asleep, so I spent the night lying next to him, afraid to move, wide awake in horrible pain, trying to figure out what I was going to do next.

The next morning when he woke up the first words that he spoke to me after calling me off from work for being "sick" were that I "owed him an apology for almost making him kill me last night." He screamed, "Do you fucking hear me bitch? Say it!" So, I did.

The next words he spoke were words that I heard every day for the next four months until I realized that if I didn't leave him, he would without a doubt kill me. "If you leave me or tell anyone that I hurt you I will kill you Nicole. I will hunt you down like a dog no matter how far you run. I will find you Nicole and I will slit your throat and you will never see your children again."

I knew without a doubt that he meant every word that he said and that once I left him, I had to be prepared to battle to stay alive.

CHAPTER 12

Living a Painful Lie

For the next 4 and a half months I told no one what was happening behind closed doors. I continued to put on an act and pretend that everything was fine in public and became a master at explaining away bruises and avoiding uncomfortable conversations.

I remember thinking that I would rather live anywhere, even a hole in the ground than in that house with him. That house that I used to love so much, that beautiful house where I had picked out the flooring, cabinets and paint colors.

That house where I had spent the past 6 years raising my children and planting a beautiful perennial garden no longer brought me anything but feelings of fear and anxiety. I remember disappearing into the basement to do laundry for as long as I could when he was home just to get away from him because he had become so unpredictable and volatile. I had become trained to be as quiet and compliant as I could be.

I no longer looked people in the eye when I talked to them because I felt ashamed and unworthy. I no longer felt comfortable expressing my opinions even at work where I knew they were valued.

After hearing his put downs and negative opinions of me for so long I had actually begun to believe that they were true. I was beaten down not just physically but emotionally, and my self-esteem was at the lowest point of my life. My confidence was gone, my sense of self was gone, and I had become a shell of the person that I used to be.

Looking back I remember that there were many times when I was talking to my Mom or coworkers or friends that I desperately wanted to tell them what was happening but I was so terrified of him and what he would do if he found out that I told someone that I became physically unable to form the words whenever I tried to verbalize them.

CHAPTER 13

Our Last Family Trip

In late August of 2009 we had a family vacation planned to go to Grand Haven which is a fun little beach town on the west side of Michigan. We had rented a place there to spend a week on Lake Michigan.

I remember knowing that one way or another this would be the last family vacation that we would ever have together so I promised myself that no matter happened I would make this the most amazing and fun filled experience for my children as possible so they could have at least one more positive memory of their childhoods and our family before everything was torn to shreds.

I remember how awful he was to me the entire vacation, how he slept the entire time I drove but got angry and slapped me when I woke him because I was lost and needed help navigating. I remember how he was constantly glaring at me with hatred and contempt. How he would do things like ask me what I wanted for dinner only to reply with "nobody gives a fuck what you want anyway" just to mess with my head.

When we were out in public he would act like the perfect husband and father and would whisper if he had something mean to say to me or felt like I had somehow stepped out of line so no one else could hear him.

Even though I knew that other people couldn't hear him I still felt so much shame and embarrassment it was hard to hold back the tears and pretend like everything was okay. I also knew if I started to cry, he would come back with his standard response, "you better not cry, or I will really give you something to cry about later."

By this point in time I absolutely despised this man that I had once loved. It took all of my self-control not to cry, argue or respond to his humiliating comments towards and about me but I wanted this last trip to be as much fun for my boys as possible. I kept reminding myself that this was the last time I would ever have to endure a trip with him and I did my best to put on a smile and make it as much fun for the boys as I could without making him suspicious.

CHAPTER 14

Do or Die

By October of 2009 I was so miserable and exhausted from constantly walking on eggshells and not knowing when he was going to blow up next or actually pull the trigger of that gun the next time it was held against my head. I knew that I had to leave.

I remember lying in bed trying to figure out a way that I could get to the gun before him the next time he became escalated so that I could protect myself. I decided to move the gun to a slightly different spot in our closet just so I would stand a chance of getting to it first.

After doing research about domestic violence over a few months' time, I had already learned that if I killed him in self-defense and nobody knew that there was domestic violence happening behind closed doors that I would never be believed, and I would likely end up in prison for the rest of my life leaving my boys without parents.

While I was in my safe pace, which was at work, I continued to do research online on how to safely leave an abusive relationship. I followed the advice that I read and began to set things in motion. I made copies of important documents like birth certificates, my marriage license, financial statements, social security letters, anything I could get my hands on easily while he was at work.

Next came my finally admitting to my mother what was really happening in my marriage and what I planned to do. She had no idea how bad things had gotten but she didn't doubt me or question my need to leave.

The next day my mom set up a checking account in both of our names so that I could change my direct deposit at work immediately because we knew it would take two weeks to process.

While he was at work, I began to take clothing items to my mother's house a little bit at a time for the boys and I so he would not notice anything major missing. I also took some pictures and other personal items that I loved and knew I would never see again after I left as was recommended in so many of the articles that I read.

I filed for a personal protection order and planned with my sister to go to her house in Canada the moment it was approved because I had no idea how he was going to react. I told no one else what was happening for two reasons. First, I didn't want anyone to slip up and accidently tell him what my plan was. Second, I was still embarrassed and felt shame for staying as long as I did.

Embarrassed because society constantly blames domestic violence victims for getting involved with abusers and for staying with them. Ashamed because people often joke about domestic violence, shame victims and hold them accountable for their own abuse and physical and emotional pain. Shame because I didn't know any better yet.

CHAPTER 15

Leaving My Life Behind

In November of 2009, on the day that my Personal Protection Order was approved I took the day off of work, loaded up my car, picked my kids up from school and drove straight to my sister Christine's house in Canada before Kevin got served with the personal protection order.

I remember trying my best to explain to my children what was happening and why. They already knew about the abuse because they had witnessed it for the past several years and it had gotten progressively worse.

I did my best to reassure them that everything was going to be okay and that we were going to look at this week as a vacation with their aunt while we figured out our next steps. I remember them having a few questions but not being overly surprised or unhappy about us leaving.

I was terrified but I had to let my boss and coworkers know what was happening and why I would be gone from work for at least a week. I was embarrassed and ashamed of what was happening behind closed doors and I was afraid that they were going to look at me differently or with less respect. I sent them an email explaining honestly what was happening and that I would let them know more as soon as I knew more.

The responses that I got were incredibly supportive and genuine about their worry for us and offers of help with whatever we needed. It was a huge relief for me to get that type of response and it gave me hope that others may respond in the same way.

I remember being so absolutely terrified that he was going to get served that order of protection and come straight to Canada to kill us. It was incredibly stressful. I could not sleep at night, I was jumpy, I was irritable, I cried and felt so completely helpless and afraid it was horrible. My sister and her husband did their best to make us feel safe and comfortable.

My ex-husband began texting, emailing and calling all of us in an attempt to talk to me. Of course, he was making promises to change, to go to rehab, to be a better person if we would just come back.

This was a complete 360 degree turn around from the person he had been just days before we left. I knew better than to believe him and too much damage had been done for me to ever want to try to make the marriage work again.

It didn't take but five days for those messages and texts to turn from apologetic to threatening. I decided to stay in Canada for another week. I also contacted my work and my kid's schools to set up safety plans in advance of us coming back to work and school when we returned.

At some point during the stay at my sister's house, my anxiety became so bad and I became so fearful of him finding us that my sister and her husband sent us to a hotel with a waterpark for a few days so the kids could be entertained and I could feel safer.

After those two weeks we returned to stay at my mother's house in Michigan. Safety plans were set up at the boy's schools and my work with my ex-husband's picture posted at every reception desk and entry point along with instructions to call 911 if and when he appeared.

CHAPTER 16

Financial Abuse

Many victims of domestic violence experience Financial Abuse at the hands of their abusers, and I was not the exception. My ex-husband always kept our finances mostly hidden from me.

We had a joint checking account for shared expenses but I always had my own checking account where my paychecks went, and I would deposit money into our joint account each month to help with expenses. He kept his personal account information hidden from me in his locked office.

Years earlier when things were good he had talked me into putting money each month into his IRA because there was a much higher interest rate than mine. We both contributed into our boy's college savings accounts each month and while we did not live an extravagant lifestyle for the most part, we were financially stable.

Once I left the relationship, he immediately withdrew all of the money from our joint checking account which had several thousand dollars in it so I would not have access to it.

Once I filed for divorce, unbeknownst to me, he stopped making my car payment and car insurance payment against court orders. There was also a court order immediately put into place stating that neither of us could withdraw any money from pensions, IRA's, joint accounts, etc. Unfortunately he did not care about court orders so he withdrew all of the money from the IRA we were both contributing to, withdrew the boys college funds as well as withdrew all of the money from his pension because he knew that Michigan Law entitled me to half of everything.

The total that he withdrew from all of our accounts after penalties was approximately $75,000.

In the midst of the divorce I found out through a credit report that my ex-husband had taken things a step further. Because he was an authorized user on a credit card I had opened up years before to pay for our patio and landscaping when we first bought our new home he was able to call the credit card company and change the contact number to his personal cell phone and the address to the mailbox facility he used for his work shipments and deliveries.

Once he did that, he took two of his credit card balances totaling $23,000 and transferred them onto the credit card that I was the primary card holder on. After numerous phone calls and complaints filed, I learned that what he did was completely legal because he was an authorized user on that card and that his $23,000 of credit card debt was now officially mine and there was nothing I could do about it.

I also learned through that credit report that he had opened up another credit card in my name and charged $5,000 on to it using that same mailbox address. After hours spent making many phone calls and faxing multiple documents of proof this card was removed from my credit report.

Although my ex-husband was ordered to pay me $850 a month in child support, I never received a dime. He refused to pay me on his own and by the time the support order finally went through the Friend of The Court because he had dragged the divorce out for more than a year, he had already lost his high paying job. This is when he began job hopping and working under the table as a means to prevent me from ever getting any child support from him.

Because he kept hiring and firing attorneys throughout our divorce my attorney was forced to start over again with each new attorney which just added costs to my attorney bill. The Judge who was handling our family court case ordered that we go to mediation despite my attorney's objections which cost $1500. That $1500 truthfully could have been better spent used as toilet paper than for mediation. Anyone with basic knowledge about domestic violence, especially a history like my case knows that mediation is not only ineffective but can often be dangerous.

Of course, he refused to cooperate or compromise on anything during mediation. After two failed sessions, the mediator let our Judge know that mediation was not going to work and our divorce was finally scheduled for a hearing.

By the time our divorce was finalized in April of 2011, my attorney fees totaled $25,000 and I now had his $23,000 of credit card debt in my name which made it my responsibility. As a consequence for his actions, the Judge gave him 5 years to pay me back the money that he had taken out of those shared accounts and his pension against court order. He was also ordered to pay me $850 a month in child support.

It has been 10 years since that order was issued and I have not received a dime in child support or of the $37,000 he was ordered to pay me back for the money he removed from our joint accounts.

My car was repossessed because he stopped making the court ordered payments. After my mother gave me a vehicle to drive, I quickly learned that I now had a ridiculously high auto insurance payment because I unknowingly went without insurance for a year. He had not been making payments as ordered by the court and my credit score was ruined. Due to his financial abuse I was eventually forced to file for bankruptcy.

All the things that he did were in an attempt to keep me from being able to leave him and stand on my own two feet. They were a display of power and control just like any other form of abuse.

Sadly, the legal system allowed him to get away with it and if I had not had a degree and a good job along with my family's support when I left, I would have had to go into a shelter if there was even a room available at the time. The alternative would have been to become homeless and I knew he would have used that against me in court when it came to winning custody of our children.

All the things that my ex-husband did to attempt to control me financially are tactics that abusers use time and time again to force their victims to come back to them or so they can have a leg up in the family court system.

It would seem that judges would be knowledgeable enough about domestic violence and the abuse cycle by now to see through these games used by abusers. Unfortunately, I often see victims lose all of their assets, go into poverty and lose custody of their children because their abusers are allowed to continue to abuse them through the legal system by Judges, Guardian Ad Litems and Court Appointed Mediators who do not have a good understanding of abuse tactics.

Abusers often hire high powered attorneys while their victims are being destroyed financially and can't afford any attorney at all. The abusers can then look like the "stable" parent and make the victim look helpless and unstable. It is heartbreaking to hear about these stories unfolding every day.

CHAPTER 17

Losing Friends

After the boys and I returned to Michigan from staying with my sister in Canada we went to stay with my Mother in Saline, Michigan for a few months before finding a rental home closer to the boy's schools.

Once I returned to Michigan, I started to notice that I was hearing less and less from several of my friends. Some of them were mutual "couple friends" of ours through sports but I thought I had close friendships with the women from that group so it was really painful for me to find out that I was no longer being invited to their group events or family parties.

Over time I received fewer and fewer text messages and phone calls from them.

I realized that it was possible that they just didn't know what to say to me after learning what had been happening behind closed doors or maybe they didn't know how to help me so instead of asking they just pulled away. I knew that it was also possible that they didn't believe me and thought I was making the abuse up, so they were choosing to no longer be my friends or even choosing my ex over me.

This made things much harder for me during that time because I was already carrying so much stress, anxiety and fear that having my friends abandon me at the same time was incredibly difficult and painful. Their pulling away from me also meant my children seeing their children less and I know that was confusing and difficult for my boys at that time.

As my ex-husband's stalking behavior increased and his threats to harm me escalated I heard even less from those friends and learned later that he was making insinuations to them or their husbands that if they were hanging out with me they may be in danger too.

I had other friends who did stand by me but told me that their other friends or family members had asked them why they were still spending time with me because they could be endangering themselves by being friends with me. I had never even thought about that being an issue so I it hit me hard to hear that. I realized that other people might also feel that being around me put them in danger and that I had now become a risk factor.

Because so many of my other friends had disappeared after I left my abuser, I found myself heavily relying on my friends and coworkers where I was working during that time for support and advice. Thankfully they were there for me and were always supportive, kind and willing to help me in any way that they possibly could.

I remember them even holding a "housewarming shower" for me because they knew that we had left our home with basically nothing but some clothes and a few pictures. That act of kindness was so incredibly powerful and touching it reminded me that there are good people in this world who really do care.

CHAPTER 18

The Stalking Begins

*Artwork by Carter Beverly, Age 6

When I first returned from my sister's house in Canada after obtaining the Personal Protection Order, I think my ex-husband thought that he could just apologize and convince me to come back. He would attempt to use our custody exchanges to talk about us getting back together, constantly call and text me to apologize for the way he had treated me and make offers to go to rehab , go to counseling and do whatever else it would take for us to be a family again.

Things began to shift again after I moved out of my Mother's house into a rental house that I could barely afford and filed for divorce. I think at that point he realized that I was not coming back. His behavior again shifted from apologetic and caring to angry and threatening.

Through the research that I did on Domestic Violence and Stalking as I was preparing to leave I had thankfully read somewhere that documenting every episode of stalking, harassment and threats was the best way to create a long enough paper trail for law enforcement and the legal system to actually help you. I began keeping a notebook with me at all times and did my best to document every incident that occurred which was very time consuming and difficult but ultimately became a life saver for me later. I tried to remember to include date, time, what occurred and whether there were any witnesses present every time something occurred. I also added if I had called the police, the responding officers name and any other information I thought may be relevant.

Keep in mind that these are only the incidents that I actually called 911 to report related to my ex-husbands threatening and stalking behavior between March 2010 and October 2011. They do not include the dozens of times he violated the PPO by walking up to me, touching me, pulling up chairs next to me at sporting events, taking pictures of me, threatening to kill me both in person and on the phone as we were still ordered to communicate regarding custody exchanges and our children.

There were also several times that he called me from outside of my home commenting on things that he noticed like cars being in my driveway, lights being on or a new wreath on my door to make sure that I knew he was still watching me.

Out of the 13 times that I made calls to 911 only two resulted in an arrest or new charges filed against my ex-husband. Officers responding to my calls at times made me feel like I was being a nuisance or that I was being dramatic by calling for help. One officer however, made me feel like I was actually listened to by taking the time to pay attention to all the details that I was telling him. As a result, he was able to see a clearer picture of what was happening. That officer, Deputy Cooper, gave me hope for the first time that someone with the power to help me cared.

*These are incidents exactly as I documented them in my ongoing log:

3/20/10: Called 911 related to Kevin twisting my arm behind my back and putting a pillow over my face during a custody exchange. Threatened that I would never see the kids again. Officers K/A responded. (PPO in place, arrest, no charges authorized by Prosecutor).

5/20/10: Called 911 after Kevin cornered my friend and I in the concession stand at my son's baseball game where we were volunteering and threatened both myself and my friend. (no arrest, no charges authorized).

5/30/2010: Kevin had the boys for his visitation and despite having a personal protection order stating that he was not allowed to come to my home he called me stating that he was there to pick up our son's baseball uniform. I told him that he was not allowed to be here but he insisted on getting the uniform. I retrieved the uniform and opened the door to hand it to my son when Kevin rushed up to the door and as if he was attempting to enter. As I shut the door he threw a lit cigarette in my face but I was able to close and double lock the door before he got inside. I called 911 and the responding Officer Cooley was able to locate him and arrest him for Domestic Violence.

6/17/10: Judge finally ordered that he surrender his 2 handguns after me requesting this multiple times since March.

7/20/10: Called 911 and played recorded conversations for responding officer, Deputy Able of Kevin stating that he was going to come to my home and slit my throat or choke me to death. That he would be waiting for me when I least expected. (PPO in place, No arrest, no charges filed by prosecutor.)

9/15/10: Called 911 after Myles, then age 9, broke down in tears suddenly and told me that his dad was using his cell phone to communicate with me during his last visit and was pretending to be him. He then shared that his Dad had hit him in the head multiple times after he ate a pop tart before weighing in for his youth football game. Myles said that his Dad then told him that if he told anyone about being hit, he would come to my house and beat me with a baseball bat and brass knuckles until my face looked like raw hamburger meat. He then asked Myles if he knew what raw hamburger meat looked like. I called 911 and officers Larper and Falls responded and Myles was interviewed by them and confirmed what he told me to police. (No arrest, no new charges filed by the prosecutor)

9/20/10: Kevin pleads guilty to domestic violence prior to jury selection from his arrest in June by Officer Cooper. He is placed on probation and released from jail.

9/20/10: I had an alarm system installed due to constant fear. I am still required to share custody and we now exchange at the police department.

12/6/10: Kevin files a motion to withdraw his plea due to having problems with employment. His motion is denied 1/10/11.

4/28/2011: Kevin approached me during a custody exchange at McDonald's as ordered by the court and said he was going to "slit my throat". I retreated back to my car and Kevin began yelling threats at me from outside of the car and banging on the window. He told me I was lucky to still be breathing and told me I was not going to live to see the kids graduate". He kept saying "if you only knew…" He then opened my vehicle door that I thought was locked and began to try to pull me out of the vehicle. I called 911 and he fled. Deputy Wild took my report and called Kevin on the phone and he said he would not come in or provide a statement. (No arrest, charges denied by prosecutor's office despite PPO still in place)

4/28/2011: I received a phone call from Child Protective Services indicating that the responding officer had called them to report that I had placed my children in danger during a custody exchange.

CHAPTER 19

Halloween 2011

On October 31, 2011, I contacted Kevin's probation officer after he was continuously calling and texting me to threaten me about an upcoming Friend of the Court hearing on his failure to pay child support. I shared that Mr. Beverly was repeatedly calling me and threatening to kill me if I did not reconcile with him. I let her know that one of Mr. Beverly's close childhood friends, Mr. Ivory had also reached out to me and stated that he was very worried about my safety as Mr. Beverly was calling him and telling him that he intended to kill me if I did not take him back. He also shared that he believed that Mr. Beverly had been at my home hiding under my deck and that I needed to be extremely cautious.

His probation officer asked me to come into the office to meet in person and while I was there Kevin was continuing to insistently call and text me. I allowed both her and her coworker to listen to him threatening me by putting my phone on speaker. His probation officer told me that she would document what she overheard and that I needed to immediately file another police report at the station which was attached to the probation department. She told me that she would call ahead and let them know that I was coming in to make a report and that she would be emailing over her documentation to them.

I walked over to the service window at the station and let them know what I had been instructed to do by my ex-husband's probation officer and that I needed to file a police report. I sat and waited for two hours in the lobby area for an officer to finally come out and talk me.

I was frustrated after waiting for so long that I was just about to leave when Deputy Ellis appeared and called me into the main office. He asked me why I was there to file a complaint. I did my best to explain the entire situation including the divorce, the stalking and his previous arrest and probation status as concisely as I could.

Deputy Ellis then turned, looked directly at me and asked, "Well, what did you do to cause him to be this upset?"

I sat in disbelief and asked him what he meant? He stated that "there were always two sides to every situation". I was absolutely stunned as I could not believe that I was actually being asked what I had done to cause my ex-husband to threaten to kill me by a trained police officer!

For some reason the Deputy looked out the window at that moment and asked what type of vehicle my ex-husband drove. I told him that my ex-husband now was driving a black Toyota. He asked me to look out the window and see if it was his car running in the parking lot and I could not believe it, but it was.

Upon seeing us looking out through the blinds, Kevin drove off. Deputy Ellis finished taking my report and stated that he would send it to the Prosecutor's office, and they would decide as to whether they would press new charges or not.

CHAPTER 20

The Chase

As I drove home from the police station, I was very anxious because I knew that Kevin was aware that I wasn't at home and was possibly headed there. I had already called the boys and reminded them to keep the doors locked and not open them for anyone until I got home.

As I was driving, I saw Kevin's vehicle sitting at The National Guard Armory entrance a few driveways down from the police station. After I drove past him, he immediately pulled out behind me and began attempting to pull up beside my vehicle.

I was completely terrified because I was sure that if he was able to get close enough, he would shoot and kill me as he had threatened to do so many times before.

I sped up and cut through a neighborhood because I thought that my best bet was to get back to the police station as quickly as possible. I called 911 and I explained to the operator what was happening, and she told me to head back to the station as safely as I could as she dispatched officers. I had to drive up onto a curb and grassy area to avoid him blocking me from turning back on to a main street.

I remember being equally afraid of being shot and killed and of hitting another car and hurting someone else as I was attempting to avoid him ramming me or pulling along side of me. I was waiting to hear shots ring out, feel a piercing pain or the force of his car hitting mine at any moment. Somehow, despite my fear, I made it back to the police station and they took another report of the incident. They called me an hour later and told me that they had sent other deputies out to look for him but were unable to locate him at that time.

Deputy Ellis suggested that I go to the Domestic Violence shelter for the night, but it was Halloween and my children were very excited to go trick or treating with friends. I was tired of letting him ruin plans for the kids and I was tired of no one doing anything to step in and help us. I headed back home filled with even more fear and anger. Once I arrived home I was able to hold it together long enough to help the kids get ready and remind them of the safety plan if anyone was to approach them or the group that they were trick or treating with.

At approximately 7 pm that evening as we were standing on the porch handing out candy to trick or treaters my friends and I saw my ex-husband drive by slowly and wave. I remember just holding my breath and again waiting for a shot to ring out or to feel the piercing of a bullet as he was driving by. I called 911 again to report what had happened.

Deputy Ellis contacted me at around midnight that night to let me know that my ex-husband had been found driving around in my neighborhood after my last 911 call and had been arrested. He shared that he had open alcohol in the vehicle, but also mentioned that no breathalyzer was done during arrest. This would have been another violation of his probation had a breathalyzer been done and documented.

During the call he asked me if it was true that Kevin was a former police officer which I found to be odd. I confirmed that he had been for few years but that that had been over 10 years ago. The officer appeared to take note and ended the call.

Once the case went to the Prosecutor's office he was charged with Aggravated Stalking. As we got close to his upcoming court date I was asked if I would be comfortable with Kevin pleading his Aggravated Stalking Charge which was a felony down to a misdemeanor Stalking Charge. I was unfamiliar with the difference in the charges or the consequences and was told by the staff at the prosecutor's office that he would have better supervision and stricter requirements if he was put on "misdemeanor Probation" than "felony Parole."

They explained that probation officers had fewer cases and could keep a closer eye on him, so I agreed.

In the end, he plead guilty to misdemeanor stalking and served a total of 60 days in jail including the time he was incarcerated during the court process. Once he plead guilty to misdemeanor stalking, he was released and ordered to continue with the same probation requirements that he had before this arrest.

Excerpt from Police Report #11052932-0004

CR No: 11052932-0001-0004 Date 10/31/2011

Contempt of Court PPO Violation

Intimidation/Stalking

Dispatch Info: The victim (Nicole Beverly) stated she has a PPO that has been served against her ex-husband/suspect (Kevin Beverly). Nicole explained that Kevin has become more unpredictable and she fears for her life because of some of the things that she has heard. On Saturday (10-29-11) Kevin's barber (close friend) Mr. Ivory called Nicole and told her Kevin was asking about getting a gun. Marcus explained to Nicole, Kevin is working at a bar as a bouncer and needs one for protection. [Not accurate]

As I was finishing the interview with Nicole I looked outside in the parking lot and observed a vehicle slowly moving through the lot. At that point I asked what Kevin drives. Nicole described a black Toyota with four doors. I then asked Nicole what Kevin looks like. Nicole stated that he is about 6'3" and about 350 pounds. I asked Nicole to look out the window to see if that was Kevin. Nicole answered that she didn't get a good look at the vehicle. [Not accurate] I walked Nicole to her vehicle out in the front parking lot and she left. About thirty seconds later Dispatch was saying over the radio Nicole was calling in saying Kevin was waiting in the entrance of the Armory which is the first driveway east of Sta2's driveway. Nicole was telling Dispatch that Kevin was following her east on S. Huron River Drive, south on Michael Dr, South on Cary Dr and then west on Textile, then north on Whittaker. Nicole explained when she

arrived back at Sta2; Kevin was driving like he wanted to pull in front of her vehicle.

While I was back at Sta2, I had dispatch find out about Kevin's vehicle which is registered to his father. Toyota 4 dr, black MI plate (6GEK95). Nicole again called Dispatch saying that she sees Kevin in that vehicle driving around her neighborhood. Sgt. A and I left Sta2. Sgt A drove south on Whittaker while I drove east on S. Huron River Dr. While I drove on HRD, I turned south on Michael Dr, and continued south on Cary Dr. As I'm south bound on Cary, I observed a dark colored vehicle north bound on Cary. I flipped back and followed the vehicle and observed it driving to the entrance of Schooner Cove and observed the vehicle driving to the club house as the vehicle turned around and hesitated, I pulled behind the vehicle. I observed the matching plate and conducted a traffic stop.

Driver Contact: I observed a large black male matching the description of Kevin Beverly seated in the driver's seat. I approached the driver and asked if he was Kevin and he said yes. After back up arrived, I had Kevin exit his vehicle. I had him place his cell phone on the roof of his vehicle and placed him under arrest for violation of PPO. Kevin stated that he was just driving in the area. Kevin states he wasn't bothering anybody. I asked him if he had contacted Nicole and he said he had not called Nicole tonight. I photographed the face of Kevin's cell phone with his number and Nicole's cell number with *67 displayed on the front.

Note: [No breathalyzer or drug screening conducted despite alcohol bottles in vehicle on Halloween night.]

Witness Statement 1: Mrs. Beverly reported that Mr. Beverly had continuously made the following comments to her over the past few months. Exact dates and times are not known. Mr. Beverly told Mrs. Beverly that if she did not take him back their children would "have no parents". Mr. Beverly told her that she had "no choice and they were going to be a happy family". Mr. Beverly has told Mrs. Beverly multiple times that he was going to "kill both her and himself". On 10/30/11, Mr. Beverly stated that there is "nothing that a judge can do to keep him away" and that a piece of paper was not going to work. On 10/31/11 Mr. Beverly called Mrs. Beverly and asked "why she had left her garage door open". Mrs. Beverly quickly checked and found her son had left the garage door open. Mrs. Beverly reports that she is fearful for her own life and the lives of her family. She reported that Mr. Beverly's close friend, Mr. Ivory has also contacted her with concerns about Mr. Beverly harming her.

Witness Statement 2: Mr. Ivory states that he is mutual friends with both Mr. And Mrs. Beverly. He stated that he recently had phone contact with Mrs. Beverly and told her several comments that were made by Mr. Beverly. Mr. Ivory provided me with the following statements made by Mr. Beverly over the past few months but exact dates and times were unknown. Mr. Beverly stated that he would "blow her (Mrs. Beverly's) brains out" if she does not take him back. Mr. Beverly stated that he would do a "murder/suicide" if Mrs. Beverly did not take him back. Mr. Beverly asked Mr. Ivory if he knew of anyone that could "take Mrs. Beverly out". Mr. Beverly asked Mr. Ivory if he could get him another gun. On 10/29/11 Mr. Beverly told him that he had to be quiet because was in her "crawl space" but exact location was unclear.

CHAPTER 21

On the Run

After his aggravated stalking charge was pled down to a misdemeanor, Kevin was released from jail. At that time, the court finally agreed to require that Kevin's visitations with the boys be supervised by a local organization. I was relieved by this change because I did not feel comfortable having the boys spend time with him unsupervised as he continued to spiral out of control.

Things were quiet for a few months. After I had gone through the entire interview and registration process with the organization assigned to supervise visitation, he refused to participate. He stated that he would not visit with his children if someone was going to be "watching his every move."

I was still not receiving any child support or payments on the money that he owed me after withdrawing the funds from all of our accounts during the divorce. By this time, I had become accustomed to living on a very limited budget, so I had not even bothered to call Friend of the Court for months.

In early October, I was surprised to receive a letter of notice from Friend of the Court that they were scheduling a hearing for November 1st related to his failure to pay child support.

On October 15, 2012 I received a phone call from an unidentified phone number and answered. It was Kevin and he was yelling at me, telling me that he knew I had reported him to Friend of the Court and because of me, he would be facing jail time if he didn't pay them $1500 by November 1st.

He then told me that, "if I knew what was good for me, I would sign off on the child support that he owed me because he was not going back to jail." I knew exactly what he meant at that moment, he meant that if I didn't sign off on the money that he owed, he would kill me. I felt a rush of fear and I hung up the phone.

Kevin continued to call and text me repeatedly over the course of the next three days. At times he would call from other phone numbers or call my boys phones and demand that they put me on the phone. He was behaving very erratically and was making statements about me letting him move in with me, telling me that he was begging me to sign off on the child support and that if I didn't, I would soon be begging him for my life.

By this time Kevin had supposedly moved to his Father's home in Oakland County and as a result was now required to report to two probation officers, one in Washtenaw County and one in Oakland County. On Thursday October 18th, the third day of repeated calls and threats I contacted Kevin's probation officer in Ann Arbor to express my fears and concerns. The probation officer asked me to come in and show me my phone so that she could see the calls and texts that I was receiving. While I was in her office, she took pictures of my phone documenting the incoming calls and text messages.

As I was talking to her I broke into tears because I could not believe that this was happening again. I was exhausted, I was afraid, and I was overwhelmed. The probation officer appeared to understand my fears and frustration and she let me know that she planned to put in an arrest warrant for his violating probation and that he would not be notified of the warrant. Because he was reporting to probation for his regular meeting date in Oakland County on Monday, October 22nd she planned on having him arrested there and communicated this with his other probation officer where he would be reporting.

We cancelled our plans to go to an apple orchard and haunted house with friends that weekend and the boys and I hunkered down in the house while Kevin continued to call and text all of our phones making negative and threatening statements. We ended up having to turn off our ringers, but the calls would just not stop.

On Monday, October 22nd I was at work trying my best to do my job but also nervously waiting for a call from Kevin's probation officer in Oakland County letting me know that he was in custody. He had begun to call my office phone and our receptionist early that morning but had stopped calling around 3 pm. I was hopeful that meant that he was now in custody and I could breathe a sigh of relief.

At 5 pm I finally received a phone call from the Oakland County probation officer. I answered the phone prepared to hear that he was in custody but instead, she uttered the words, "I'm sorry but he fled arrest while they were trying to put cuffs on him." She went on to explain that they had not cuffed him before telling him that I had filed a complaint and that he was going to be arrested for violating his Probation conditions. She went on to say that he had run out of the building through the back parking lot employee entrance and that they had contacted all of the police stations in the area with a Lookout order to locate him and his vehicle.

The probation officer stated that since they were unaware of Kevin's whereabouts, I should contact my local police and make them aware of the situation and do what was necessary to ensure our safety.

I sat at my desk feeling immobilized. I could not believe that he was able to flee arrest and I knew that now he was going to be even angrier with me than before and would only have more motivation to attempt to hunt me down and harm me as he had promised to do so many times before.

I somehow found my composure and called both my mother and the Washtenaw County Sheriff's Department to arrange a Stand By Officer while I went to my house and gathered enough clothing and personal items for the boys and I to stay somewhere else for at least a few days.

On my way home, I received a phone call from an unknown number and I thought that it might be the police or probation officer calling me, so I answered. It was Kevin and he was angry. He stated, "Why did you set me up bitch?" After I hung up the phone he continued to call, text and leave threatening voicemail messages. I was truly terrified.

We decided as a family that it made the most sense for the three of us to stay in three different places that were with safe adults so that we would not all be together if he found us. I contacted the boy's schools to create an updated safety plan and met with my supervisor and our receptionist to create a new plan should he show up at my job to carry out his threats to kill me.

CHAPTER 22

5 Days of Fear

On Wednesday, October 24th I made the decision that I needed to go and purchase a firearm for my personal protection and obtain a license to carry a gun on my person. I never imagined that I would reach the point of actually needing to do this but at this point I knew that I had no other choice than to take my family's safety and protection into my own hands.

I went to the Sheriff's Department to obtain a permit to purchase a firearm. A few minutes after leaving my phone rang and I answered it hoping it was someone calling me with an update about Kevin's whereabouts. The second I picked up the phone Kevin began screaming at me, saying that I "had set him up" and that I must call his probation officer and tell her to drop all of the charges immediately. He instructed me that I needed to tell the probation officer that I was just upset with him for not paying child support. He went on to yell at me and instructed me that if "I knew what was good for me", I would tell them that I wanted him back in my life and had made a huge mistake. He demanded that I tell them that I wanted him to be allowed to have phone contact with me again.

Kevin went on to tell me that if I did not make this phone call and take care of everything within the next 30 minutes, he would hunt me down and kill me. He said that he had three guns hidden in different locations and planned to shoot me if I didn't follow through with his demands.

I was absolutely panicked and didn't know what to do so I drove straight to his probation officer's office in Ann Arbor to share with her what was happening. I was an absolute wreck by this point and immediately broke into tears upon entering the office. I could not believe that this was happening and that he had been able to escape arrest so easily. It was unbelievable to me that professionals would tell a perpetrator that their victim had reported a new crime and then just allow him to run out of the building!

The probation officer suggested that I file another police report in Washtenaw County about the new threats, so I headed back to the Sherrif's Department and filed another police report. As I was making the police report the deputy taking my report shared that there had been no Lookout order issued by the probation office in Oakland County as she had told me she had done and that he could find no evidence of any new charges related to my ex-husband fleeing arrest in Oakland County. I was shocked. How could he not be facing new charges after fighting off Probation Officers attempting to arrest him after threatening to kill me? The officer also told me that he would be forwarding his report to the Washtenaw County Prosecutor's office for their review.

My next stop was a gun store in Westland, Michigan that had been recommended by a friend. After speaking to the sales associates extensively and shooting three separate handguns to see which I was most comfortable with, I purchased a Smith and Wesson 9mm handgun. I also signed up for a handgun safety and license to carry class beginning in a few days.

I contacted my children and the families they were staying with to give them updates and make sure that everyone was okay as often as possible. My employer graciously moved me into another building that my ex-husband was unaware of so that I would not have to take any further time off of work.

On October 25th, I was notified that the Washtenaw County Prosecutor had reviewed the police report and authorized a SWAT team to go looking for my ex-husband as a result. Kevin continued to call and text me both on my cell phone and at work continuously.

On October 26th I was notified that the SWAT team had been unsuccessful in locating my ex-husband and that the Prosecutor had authorized the US Marshalls to locate him as they realized how high my lethality risk was at this point.

I was still naïve at that point in time, so I expected that everything would happen very quickly like it does on the crime tv shows and that my husband could be tracked down easily with cell phone towers.

A few hours later, a detective assigned to the case contacted me and let me know that they had obtained a warrant for Kevin's cell phone company and were finally able to begin tracking his phone.

That evening after what felt like days, I finally received a phone call from the detective indicating that my ex-husband had finally been located at a hotel in Dearborn, MI and had been taken into custody.

After 5 days of hiding, running and living in intense fear we could finally go home.

CHAPTER 23

The Plea

By the time the new Aggravated Stalking case made it to court in March of 2013, I learned that he had agreed to plead guilty to the charges as long as he received a COBBS agreement from the Judge that would allow him to be released from jail after the five months' time he had served waiting for a court date. He would then be placed on parole supervision instead of probation and be right back out on the street.

I was furious when I learned this information because no one had even consulted with me to find out if I was okay with this agreement. I could not believe they were going to simply just release him back onto the streets after he had fled arrest and continued to threaten and torment me for 5 straight days.

The victim advocate assigned to my case suggested that I go to the court hearing and read a victim impact statement expressing to the judge exactly what my concerns and fears were.

By this point in time I felt like I had absolutely nothing to lose, so I decided to face my abuser in court and ask the judge to reconsider his offer. I was incredibly nervous, but I faced my fears and stood before the courtroom and read the following statement out loud.

Honorable Judge D.E.S 4/10/2013

Dear Sir,

My name is Nicole Beverly. I am forty years old the mother of two young boys and a victim of domestic violence. I am also a licensed social worker with the Ypsilanti School District. I have struggled for the past 5 years to provide my children with a stable home environment. Our life has not been easy financially or emotionally due to the

mental illness and drug addiction of my ex-husband Kevin Beverly and his constant violent threats to our family.

For the past five years I have lived every day in fear for my safety and that of my children. We have been physically assaulted and mentally abused by this violent man. For the second time, Mr. Beverly is incarcerated in the Washtenaw County Jail where he continues to make threats of violence against us. In a recent court appointed anger management session he reportedly boasted to the group that they should watch for him on TV to see what he will do to me when he is released. I am terrified of this man and what he will do to me and my children. I have been beaten, held hostage with a gun and run off of the road by this man. Kevin Beverly is mentally ill and will not seek treatment. He has abused alcohol for several years which only enhances his rage.

I am appealing to you for help. I have had support from the prosecutor's office and law enforcement, but Kevin Beverly is still mentally ill and a threat to my family when and if he is released. I understand that he has plead guilty and you have agreed to some special arrangement for his release. Please advise me of any special arrangement that I can make with you to ensure that we are safe if only for the full one-year sentence. It does not serve anyone, my children, my family or myself to have Kevin Beverly back on the streets looking to avenge his delusional belief that killing me will improve his life.

I am struggling to keep everything together for my two boys. They are the reason that I am appealing to you today. I can't imagine their life if anything happens to me. Is Washtenaw County going to be responsible for raising them once Mr. Beverly kills me? Please consider Myles Beverly, 13 years old and Carter Beverly, 9 years old as you make your determination in regards to sentencing for Mr. Beverly.

Thank you for your kind consideration,

Nicole Renee Beverly

After reading my statement the Judge gave Kevin the opportunity to speak. Kevin stood up and smiled at me, then went on to say how much he loved me and that this was "just a misunderstanding." The Judge interrupted him and told him that it was time for him to stop making excuses and accept responsibility for his actions if he wanted to keep his plea deal.

Kevin continued to explain that he never had any intention of hurting me and that this was happening because I was upset about the divorce and the child support he had failed to pay.

At this point the Judge stopped Kevin from speaking and told him that it was this type of behavior that let him know that he was still not accepting responsibility for his actions. The Judge then withdrew his offer of a Cobb's agreement that would have put him right back on the street and scheduled sentencing for a few weeks out.

Despite how terrifying and difficult it was for me to stand up and speak in court that day, I was glad that I had taken a chance and stood up for myself and my children.

At sentencing a few weeks later, I anxiously held my breath as the Judge stated that Kevin was being sentenced to serve "15 months up to 5 years" in prison with time served. This meant that the soonest he could be released would be in 12 months'. One entire year. An entire year of not dealing with constant threats and harassment. One whole year of not having to look over my shoulder and hopefully being able to sleep at night.

I felt like a dark cloud had just been lifted.

CHAPTER 24

Dark Thoughts

The two and a half years that I was being stalked and threatened by my ex-husband were incredibly difficult. He would call me and start conversations calmly about the custody exchanges that the courts were forcing me to do but would quickly escalate to all of the different ways that he was going to kill me because I would not come back. He loved telling me that someday he would be hiding in my house and I would not know it until he came out of hiding in the middle of the night to slit my throat.

It understandably became very difficult for me to sleep at night. When I first left, I could not afford a home alarm system because he had taken so many of our assets and left me in financial devastation. I remember putting the $2.00 alarms from Home Depot on every door and window that I thought he could get into just so that I would have a head start to escape the house if I heard one of them go off. I slept with Mace and wasp spray next to my bed every night before I purchased and trained with my firearm.

I have never shared this with anyone before this moment, typing this today, that there came a point in 2012 that I was so certain that my ex-husband was going to kill me that I actually wrote letters to both of my boys telling them goodbye and expressing how much I loved them and hid them in a box so that they would always have something from me to keep and remember me by.

I wanted them to know how hard I fought for them and that nothing in the world mattered to me more than them. I also created funeral instructions including where the letters were hidden and created a funeral playlist on my Spotify account of songs that I would want played during my funeral.

I made my family and friends promise me that if he killed me, they would sue the State of Michigan, the police and the family court for failing to protect me and would continue to help other victims and advocate in my name.

During the darkest of times after the legal system had let me down repeatedly, I contemplated committing suicide. I thought about how I could make it look like an accident so that my boys wouldn't know that I had made the decision to leave them behind and so they could get my life insurance benefits, social security insurance income and could live safely with one of my family members.

At that time suicide felt like it may have been a better option than living in constant fear. Sadly, in many ways I felt like killing myself was the best way to protect my children. If I took myself out of the equation, they would be safer because he would have finally won, and I would be gone for good which is what he ultimately wanted.

It is incredibly difficult and painful for me to look back and admit this. At that point in time however, that was my reality and the reality that I am sure many other victims have experienced when they are dealing with constant harassment by their abusers. I'm sure even more have felt this sense of hopelessness after they are let down by the legal system that is supposed to protect them time and time again.

I am so thankful now that my will to live and see my children grow up won the battle. I truly understand how many victims of domestic violence and stalking, especially those without a circle of support decide that suicide is the best way to protect their families or end their own personal torment when no one with the power to help them does and that breaks my heart.

If anyone reading this book has reached the point where you are contemplating taking your own life, please hold on and know that there is hope.

If you are or begin to have thoughts of suicide or self-harm please call the National Suicide Hotline (1-800-273-8255) and get resources that can help you find your way back through the darkness.

CHAPTER 25

Parole is Granted

Since my ex-husband's original sentence for his stalking charge was officially documented as "15 months up to five years" it should not have surprised me that he was immediately approved for Parole at the 15-month mark in February 2014. I must remember however that I was still very naïve at that time and still had some hope that our legal system was designed to protect victims and keep them safe.

I was shocked to learn that he had been approved for parole and would be released in just a few weeks' time after completing his court ordered classes at the Detroit Re-Entry Center. I was shocked because I had been told by victim services just a few months earlier that he had been in a physical altercation with another inmate, had been found with a weapon in his cell, had attempted to hire someone to kill me less than a year before and had refused to participate in any of his court ordered classes during his incarceration.

I remember feeling like there was a clock ticking down in my head, counting the minutes I had left of freedom. I knew that I only had a few weeks left of peace and not constantly having to look over my shoulder. I began to take in and appreciate every walk I could take, every night I could sleep peacefully and every moment of joy and happiness I had left before his release date. I knew that my life was about to change dramatically.

CHAPTER 26

A Flash of Hope

A few weeks after I received notice that my ex-husband had been approved for parole and was transferred to the step-down facility in Detroit, MI, I received another unexpected phone call from law enforcement.

I was just pulling into the parking lot at work when I received the call. The woman on the other end of the line was apologetic and I could tell that she was unsure of how to initiate a difficult topic, "Ms. Beverly" she started, "I am one of the Victim Advocates within the Michigan Parole Department and I am calling you to deliver some difficult news regarding your ex-husband." I held my breath as I prepared for her to tell me that he had somehow died in prison and how I was going to break the news to my boys.

Instead, she paused then followed with "a few inmates from the prison your ex-husband was just transferred from have come forward stating that your ex-husband plans to kill you and your children as soon as he is released from his current step-down program." Long pause, "They have also shared that he may be attempting to hire other inmates to kill you and your children."

I sat in silence unsure of how to respond or understand what this meant. She continued, "Since your ex-husband has already been transferred to the Detroit Re-Entry Center (DRC), we are going to be completing an investigation and determine if his parole status will be revoked based on this new information. She added that, "Two of the inmates have completed written statements about their concerns and will be meeting with the prison warden to be interviewed."

For some reason I knew that I had to get copies of those letters for documentation so I asked and was told that she would find out if that was possible and get back with me. She never did. She stated that she would notify me of an update once the parole board made their decision.

I sat silently stunned in the parking lot for several minutes trying to take in the information that she had just shared before going in to work and pretending like I had not just received this very disturbing news. I had recently started a new job, so my new coworkers were unaware of my personal life and how extreme the situation with my ex-husband was. This was not the way I wanted to introduce that topic.

I had heard too many stories about victims of domestic violence and stalking getting fired from their jobs because of their abuser's actions causing fear in their coworkers or their employers seeing them as too high risk to continue working for them so I understandably didn't feel safe sharing information with people that I did not yet know.

As I processed the information I wasn't at all surprised that he still planned to kill me when he was released in just a few short months because he had told me hundreds of times that he was going to kill me and all of the different ways that he planned to do it. However, I was honestly shocked and sickened that he was now saying that he was planning on killing our children too.

I never imagined that he would ever consider murdering our children. In fact, it had never entered my mind up until that moment but once I finally received copies of those statements written by the two inmates that had come forward, I knew that the danger of him harming them was very real.

The truth is that he knew the way to cause me the most pain and despair would be to harm my children in front of me. My life meant nothing to me compared to the lives of my two amazing children and that is something that he has always known about me. I already knew that he was sick and twisted and had plans to kill me, but this news was terrifying to me because I knew that it was true and now, my biggest fear had been confirmed. My boys were at risk too.

Letter from Inmate #1 (AM)

My name is AM and I lock in 69-3-B behind Mr. Beverly and I personally heard Mr. Beverly state that he wanted to get out of prison kill his wife and kids. The things (statements) I'm about to write are true and honest. Mr. Beverly has said several times that he hates his wife and I guess in this type of environment that would seem to be normal but as time went on it became more often that he would say that and the statement began to come out more aggressively until he finally said "I can't wait to get out and kill that bitch".

I looked at him like he was crazy but for some odd reason I felt that he was serious and not only that he continued to say "I'm going to kill the kids too". And that's truly when I knew he was messed up in the head. He said "I'm going to get her and the kids together, I'm going to kill the kids in front of her, make her watch and then I'm going to kill her slow".

This is not something a sane man would say so out of doing the right thing for the right reason, I brought this to my ARUS (Mr. Able) attention, because I've read about men getting out of prison and killing his girlfriend, kids, family, etc. And I didn't want that to happen to that family when there was something we could have done to help them.

Ps. Please help that man and his family.

Sincerely, AM

Letter from Inmate #2 (SH)

One Day back in February I returned to the cube where I lock, and I overheard Prisoner Beverly talking to some other prisoners on how he was going to kill his wife because she put him in here. He also said he was going to kill his kids first and make his wife watch and then kill her slowly. It's been said that he has told this to a lot of prisoners here. I'm only saying something because I have kids too and I don't want to see anything happen to them.

—SH

CHAPTER 27

Hope Grows

I had anxiously been waiting an update from the parole department or Jackson Prison about the written statements turned in by the two inmates housed with him at Jackson Prison about my ex-husband's plans to kill my children in front of me before torturing me to death when I received an unexpected call on March 11th, 2013 from a Detective at the Michigan State Police post in Wayne County.

The detective that contacted me from the Taylor State Police post informed me that two inmates at the Detroit Re-Entry Center had come forward stating that my ex-husband had recently offered them $50,000 to kill myself and my children as they were scheduled for release before him.

I was confused at first as I thought he was talking about the same inmates at Jackson Prison that had come forward just days earlier about my ex-husbands plans to kill me himself. I asked for clarification, "Excuse me.... Are you talking about the inmates from Jackson prison who put statements into writing a few days ago about my ex-husband killing my children and then torturing me to death?". He replied cautiously, "No, I'm not aware of that information."

He went on to say that "These two inmates were reportedly on the bus with your ex-husband during transfer from Jackson Prison to the Detroit Re-entry Center. They claim that during the bus transfer your ex-husband inquired about needing someone to kill his ex-wife and children."

I sat in confused silence still not fully understanding that these were actually two new individuals that had come forward. I explained to him that I had been contacted a few days ago by the parole department about the inmates that had come forward at Jackson prison and about the previous attempt to hire attempt in Washtenaw County. This detective was not aware of either of these incidents. I was having a very hard time understanding how there could be no information in the State Police or Correction System about either of these previous attempts to hire and/or the threats on our lives.

The detective explained to me that these two inmates at the Detroit Re-Entry Center were putting their statements into writing and had indicated that they were possibly willing to wear a wire in order to get enough information for new charges against my ex-husband. He explained that he was planning to go interview them the next morning and would get back with me once he had an update.

Again, I found those same three emotions rising inside of me. Anxiety, fear and hope. The hope in me was saying this time with four different inmates coming forward with information we will definitely get new charges issued against him.

Excerpt from Police Report #020-0000934-14

Date: Friday, March 14, 2014 Incident#020-000934-14

On March 11, 2014 I interviewed the parolee/witness Tryone Johnson this date at approximately 0920 hrs. Johnson was reluctant to be interviewed regarding this incident though he ultimately agreed to talk to me. Johnson advised that he first met the suspect BEVERLY on the "bus" from Jackson Prison to DRC two weeks prior. Johnson could not remember the exact date that he transferred. He continued that he did not know the suspect's name, but positively identified Beverly by his prison identification picture. He advised that everyone in BEVERLY'S housing unit at DRC called him "Big B".

Johnson advised that while they were riding the bus from Jackson to DRC, BEVERLY began talking about how much he hated his ex-wife and children. He allegedly told Johnson that he wanted to kill them all. He then began asking Johnson "weird questions". Johnson gave one example: BEVERLY asked if he thought he could get away with murdering his ex-wife because he (BEVERLY) would have to wear a GPS locator while on Parole, which would show he was near her at the time of the planned murder. Johnson indicated this questioning led to BEVERLY asking him (Johnson) if he would kill his ex-wife and children. BEVERLY allegedly offered to pay Johnson $50,000 dollars to do so.

Johnson indicated he might have been willing to kill BEVERLY'S ex-wife; however he did not think that BEVERLY had the money to pay him. Johnson also said that he was disturbed that BEVERLY wanted his children killed too. Johnson advised that he did not think that was "right". He advised he ultimately decided to report the incident because he did not want the children to be harmed.

I asked Johnson if anyone else was on the bus at the time. He advised that his friend and fellow parolee Marvin Poole was sitting with them throughout the bus ride. Johnson stated he had known Poole since they were young and that they had grown up in the same neighborhood in Saginaw.

Johnson advised that they were sitting near the front of the bus and no one else was around. He clarified that there were other prisoners on the bus, but BEVERLY was talking quietly so no one else could hear. I asked Johnson to describe the seating arrangement. He advised it was a smaller size bus with bench seats that all faced the center. He indicated he was seated on the driver's side bench while BEVERLY was seated on the bench across from him. He advised that Poole was seated next to him. He estimated that the next closest prisoner was about two feet away.

Johnson claimed BEVERLY allegedly offered to pay them both $50,000 dollars in exchange for killing his ex-wife. BEVERLY told him he did not care how it was done, but wanted his ex-wife to watch the children die first to maximize her suffering. Johnson shrugged and mumbled unintelligibly when I asked him what his reaction was to this.

Johnson stated BEVERLY was then assigned to the same housing unit as him and Poole. Over the next week, BEVERLY talked constantly about wanting to kill his ex-wife and children as well as his ex-wife, her boyfriend and children. Johnson said BEVERLY was obsessed with her and would not talk about anything else. He advised BEVERLY would routinely approach him and Poole while they were sitting in the common area of the housing unit to talk about killing his wife. He advised BEVERLY did not talk to any of the other parolees because the three of them "hit it off" and had become friends. Johnson stated BEVERLY stayed in his room when he was not talking to them and did not socialize with anyone. He advised BEVERLY did not solicit anyone else regarding murdering his wife.

Johnson advised that he and Poole ultimately refused to murder BEVERLY's ex-wife. I asked why he waited so long to report BEVERLY's activities. Johnson stated he reported it to a counselor "about two days ago". He shrugged his shoulders when I asked him why he waited so long to report BEVERLY. Johnson advised he could not read or write and declined to provide a written statement.

I interviewed parolee/witness Poole this date at approximately 1025 hrs. Poole advised he understood the reason for the interview, but initially refused to participate. He stated he would not make any statements unless he received preferential treatment from DRC. He specifically demanded early placement in one of the training programs he was required to take before he was released on parole. Poole was told he would not be given anything in exchange for his statement. Poole continued to make demands, however he eventually began to talk about his contacts with BEVERLY.

Poole advised he first met BEVERLY in the housing unit at DRC. He insisted he had never seen or met BEVERLY before that. He advised BEVERLY approached him and Johnson while they were sitting in the housing unit. He indicated they struck up a conversation which led to a friendship. Poole only knew BEVERLY as "Big B". BEVERLY almost immediately began talking about his ex-wife and how much he hated her. He told Poole and Johnson he wanted to kill her and her boyfriend.

Poole advised BEVERLY then tried to hire them to kill his ex-wife for him. Poole indicated he offered them $50,000 to kill his ex-wife and her boyfriend. He allegedly told them he did not care how they did it. Poole claimed he told BEVERLY to stop talking about it and that he would not kill BEVERLY'S ex-wife. He advised he did not think BEVERLY had the $50,000. He further stated he would often see BEVERLY walking around the housing unit trying to hire people to kill his ex-wife. He then amended this and indicated BEVERLY told people he wanted to kill his ex-wife. Poole insisted he could not remember anything else about the incident.

I asked him if BEVERLY ever mentioned killing his children. Poole stated BEVERLY never stated he wanted to kill his children or to have them killed. I asked him why he waited so long to report the incident. Poole shrugged and did not answer.

CHAPTER 28

Hope Fades... Again

Two more days went by while I continued to try to work as well as parent my children with the weight of the world on my shoulders while pretending like nothing unusual was going on. I could only tell my mother and closest friends what was happening because I didn't want to risk anyone contacting him and giving him any heads up about the investigations. I also didn't want to instill any fear in my children who had already been through so much.

When I finally heard back from the detective at the Taylor State Police Post a few days later I did not receive the news I was hoping for. He called me as I returned to my office from running a therapy group with students. I sat down at my desk with anticipation and hope about hearing some good news but instead his words almost broke me.

He stated that he was calling to give me an update on the case and that "unfortunately, there was miscommunication between the state police, Jackson Prison and the Detroit Re-entry Center and that my ex-husband had been picked up at 6 am and taken back to Jackson Prison the same morning that he was planning to go out and interview the inmates at the Re-entry Center and discuss having them wear a wire to get recorded evidence."

The detective continued "Unfortunately your ex-husband was told that he was being taken back yesterday morning for another parole hearing due to several inmates coming forward with information about him intending to harm you." I sat in silence waiting for him to tell me how they were going to fix this. How they were going to make this right? How they were going to help keep us safe?

After what felt like 2 minutes of complete silence I asked "So what is the plan? These are the 3rd and 4th inmates that have come forward with information about his attempts to hire someone to kill me or plans to kill me and my children himself. What happens now?"

"There is really nothing more I can do here in Wayne County." he stated. "Your ex-husband has already been transferred back to Jackson County, so I am closing out this case and it is the State Police in Jackson County's responsibility to investigate moving forward."

I sat in stunned silence feeling heat rising up my neck and cheeks as I desperately tried to hold back my tears. I seriously could not believe the words that I was hearing. How could this possibly be happening again? How could there not be better communication between the prison system and the Michigan State Police when an entire family's life was at risk? How was he getting away with this again?

Any feelings of hope that I had previously felt slowly drained out of my body and were replaced with anger, frustration and sadness. My abuser kept proving to me that he still had power and control over me even from prison just as he had promised to do if I ever left him or told anyone about his abuse. And the worst part was that the system just continued to enable him, let me down and not seem to care. I remember feeling so alone, afraid and helpless at that moment. It was a feeling that I would not wish on anyone.

Excerpt from Police Report #020-0000934-14

Date: Friday, March 14, 2014 Incident#020-000934-14

On March 11, 2014 I responded to the DRC and met with Operations Supervisor Black at 0900 hrs. Black identified the suspect as KEVIN BEVERLY. Black advised that BEVERLY had just been transferred to the DRC on February 27, 2014. He explained BEVERLY was required to participate in several training courses at DRC prior to being released on Parole. He stated BEVERLY had been sentenced to prison due to a conviction of aggravated stalking of his former wife, NICOLE BEVERLY.

Black was notified of BEVERLY'S attempts to solicit the murder of his former wife by BEVERLY'S parole counselor Susan Wood. Wood learned of BEVERLY'S activities from the two parolees he allegedly tried to hire to murder NICOLE. She had no personal knowledge of his activities.

Black advised BEVERLY had been removed from the DRC and sent back to Jackson at 0600 hrs this date. He indicated he did not know why MDOC had transferred him prior to my initiating an investigation.

Contact other agencies:

Supervisor Black advised MDOC was aware of BEVERLY'S activities and they were conducting their own investigation. He stated the investigations unit for MDOC in Lansing was monitoring the situation.

I contacted the Washtenaw County Sheriff Office and briefed Detective Newburg regarding the interviews. He advised he would pass the information to the original OIC, and Desk Sergeant and I provided the same information to the Assistant Prosecutor.

I advised D/Sgt. Clarke (MSP Jackson) of the situation. He advised he was already aware of it. Because the suspect was transferred back to MDOC's Jackson Facility before an investigation could be conducted in Wayne County, the incident was turned over to MSP Jackson for possible follow up.

Status:

Tot other police department

Investigated by Detective Douglas #19

CHAPTER 29

Detective Clarke

Once my ex-husband was transported back to Jackson Prison for a Parole Review the case became the responsibility of the Jackson State Police. Weeks went by and I heard nothing. I called and left several messages at the Jackson State Police Post requesting information but never received a return phone call.

I reached out to Anna Slawson, my former Washtenaw County Prosecutor again who said she would find out which detective the case had been assigned to and get back with me once she had more information. After a few days she instructed me that she had called the post and spoken with a Detective Clarke who was reportedly a newly appointed detective. Detective Clarke had told her that he was unaware that the case had been assigned to him. Once Anna explained that it indeed was assigned to him according to his supervisor, he said that he would complete the investigation as soon as possible.

After another week went by with no information, no one responding to my phone calls or emails my frustration continued to grow. My mother and I decided that since no one was responding to my calls and messages that we would go to them and attempt to get someone at the police post to give us some answers.

When we arrived at the police post we asked to speak to Detective Clarke who was in charge of the investigation and happened to be there when we arrived. Once the receptionist called him out to the front and we explained who we were, he very reluctantly agreed to meet with me but would not allow my mother to come back to the conference room with us to talk. I found that very odd especially considering the fact that I was the victim in this case, but since I was no longer intimidated or afraid to talk to police officers by this time,

I simply said "no problem" and headed back to the conference room with him alone.

Initially his tone with me was very cold and dismissive as I was asking him for updates about the investigation on my ex-husband and his attempts to hire inmates to kill me at the Detroit Re-entry Center. I also asked for information about what follow up had been done with the inmates that had written the letters about my ex-husband's threats to kill my children in front of me then torture me to death.

Detective Clarke sat down, looked me in the eye and explained that "Prison is a very bad place to be and that people often say things they don't mean." I replied with "yes and living your life in fear of a man who has attempted to hire at least three people to kill you from prison after stalking you for two years is also a very bad place to be." Without missing a beat, he shared that he understood but that "prison a very, very difficult place to be."

I asked him if he was aware of the previous attempt to hire in Washtenaw County. He indicated that he was not aware of that information as he does not have access county to county of police reports. I inquired as to how this could not all be a part of my ex-husbands prison record by this point because it seemed absolutely preposterous to me that there wouldn't be a better way for vital information like this to be shared when people's lives were at stake.

At this point Detective Clarke got up and shared that he was going to go and get my Mother to join us, so I'd be more comfortable. I again thought that was strange since I was feeling very comfortable, but clearly, he was not.

Once my mother arrived in the room, I caught her up to speed and we asked Detective Clarke if he planned to do any further investigation into the case. He explained that he had already gone and interviewed my ex-husband at the prison and based on "Kevin's body language and mannerisms", this newly appointed detective made the determination that he was telling the truth and that my ex-husband really had no plans to kill me nor had he offered people money to kill me. In fact, he said that he was so calm they even "joked around a bit". I sat in utter silence and outrage as I let this all sink in. Body language? Mannerisms? Joking around? I could not believe what I was hearing. He was basing his opinions purely on body language observed during an hour-long interview. He had not requested a psychological evaluation, nor had he consulted with the prison psychiatrist for more information or a more informed opinion.

I then asked Detective Clarke if he planned on interviewing the inmates that had come forward with written statements about my ex-husband's threats to kill my children in front of me before torturing me to death upon his release from prison. The Detective stated that he "did not feel it necessary after his interview with my ex-husband" as he believed him to be telling the truth and did not believe he was attempting to solicit anyone to kill me. He then went on to say that "people can say whatever they want to about wanting to kill other people and that it is not a crime".

I tried my best to explain the history of violence, stalking and lethality risk and did everything I could but get down on my hands and knees and plead with this man to take these threats and attempts by my ex-husband to hire someone to kill me more seriously, to complete a real investigation, but it was quickly obvious that he had no interest in doing so. Before I left the room however, he did give me copies of the two letters written by the two inmates at Jackson Prison that I had not been able to get from anyone else.

I was again absolutely devastated and felt completely let down by the system. No one was listening. No one was taking this seriously. No one that had the power to help me cared. Before I left, I handed him an invitation to my upcoming speaking engagement about Domestic Violence at Eastern Michigan University and simply said sarcastically "Thanks so much for your concern and thorough investigation."

Except from Police Report #013-0001711-14

Date: April 4, 2014 #013-0001711-14

[SOLICITATION TO COMMIT MURDER]

I learned in March of 2014 that an unknown inmate was threatening to kill his ex-wife and children. I learned this from the Inspector at the Parnall Correctional Facility. The Inspector had received two "kites" from two different inmates about this. The inspector also told me the inmate, who I later learned to be Kevin BEVERLY, had been moved to the Detroit Reentry Center. He also had allegedly attempted to hire two inmates at the Detroit Reentry Center to kill his ex-wife and children.

D/Sgt. Donaldson, MSP Second District, conducted an investigation in Wayne County. He determined that the witnesses were not credible. He turned this investigation over to me, but I did not realize this until April of 2014. I was contacted in early April of 2014 by the Washtenaw County Prosecutor's Office because they were concerned about the status of this investigation.

I went to the G. Robert Cotton Correctional Facility on 04-04-14 to interview BEVERLY. BEVERLY was initially very evasive and difficult during the interview. After approximately an hour he opened up. The entire interview lasted on hour and thirty-nine minutes.

BEVERLY denied ever saying that he would kill his wife or children. He denied saying that he wanted them dead. He denied attempting to hire anyone to kill them.

Based on his responses and body language, I do not believe that BEVERLY attempted to solicit a murder. I do believe that he probably made a statement to the effect that he wished his wife was dead. In fact, when I told him my beliefs he smiled and did a half shrug, as if agreeing.

Regardless, there is no information regarding a solicitation for murder in Jackson County. I do not believe that BEVERLY committed a solicitation for murder anywhere.

This incident is closed as unfounded.

D/Sgt Clarke #10

CHAPTER 30

Finding Nicole

When I finally left my abuser in 2009, I was just the shell of the person I had once been. I could no longer look people in the eye for more than a few seconds during conversations. Whenever someone asked me what I liked to do for fun, I honestly had no answers. I no longer recognized myself in the mirror which is a very eerie feeling that almost feels like you are an outside observer looking in.

The reality is that when someone tells you something about yourself day after day you eventually begin to believe it. Towards the end of our relationship, my abuser constantly told me that I was lazy, fat and ugly. He told me that I was a stupid bitch, that no one cared about my opinions and that I would never find someone to love me again. He told me these things as often as possible so that I would be too broken to leave him. This was another form of power and control that he used to make me believe that I could not make it on my own, that no one would ever respect me and that I would never find someone that truly loved me.

I was in pure survival mode before leaving. My only goals day to day were to simply wake up and drag myself out of bed, take care of my children, go to work and not upset him. There was no fun, no joy, no laughter and nothing to look forward to.

After I left, my abuser still had power and control over me for quite some time because we were sharing custody of our boys and I was forced to communicate with him and see him at custody exchanges and he made those things as difficult and stressful for me as he possibly could. He would do things like drive off with the kids as I was pulling up to pick them up. He would then call me and say that I had been a minute late so he would meet me at the gas station but refuse to tell me which gas station for at times several hours. It was a game that he liked to play to remind me that he still had ways of harming me.

Because I had been unhappy and depressed for so long in our relationship I had put on a significant amount of weight. Food became one of the few things that brought me any type of enjoyment. I was having constant back pain to the point that I went to have nerve block injections and was taking pain medication regularly. I was too exhausted physically and emotionally to move my body to work out. At that point in time, I think it is fair to say that I no longer cared about myself at all.

The longer that I was out from under his hold, the more I noticed myself feeling less tired and more motivated to get things done. I started to feel like I could breathe again for the first time in a very long time. I began to listen to music again and read books that I had been wanting to read. I began looking at different social media pages for victims of domestic violence and how to overcome abuse. It was incredibly helpful for me to read other people's stories and to know that I wasn't alone in what I had been through and that there was hope that I could one day be strong and happy again like these other survivors I was reading about.

As my energy level continued to increase, I decided that I would sell my wedding ring and with the money buy myself an elliptical trainer so that I could begin to exercise and improve my health. I realized that I actually enjoyed working out while listening to music and that my mood and sleep began to improve even more. A secondary benefit was that I began to lose the weight that I had gained while I was trapped in that volatile and toxic relationship.

As I became stronger both physically and mentally, I began to set firmer boundaries with my ex-husband. As his threats and stalking behavior increased, I did my best to take my power back by calling the police and reporting when he violated the protection order. I refused to speak to him if it wasn't directly related to custody exchanges or a serious issue related to the children as our divorce papers stated.

I continued to visit domestic violence support pages on Facebook and eventually began to message and form online friendships with other survivors from across the nation. It was so amazing to connect with other people who were going through the same thing that I was and had similar experiences. In 2014, I attended a Domestic Violence Survivor retreat held by the organization Break The Silence Against Domestic Violence and there I connected with even more amazing survivors, many whom I still communicate with regularly today.

In 2013 I began to attend Self Defense and kick boxing classes and over time I found that I felt the most comfortable with Krav Maga which is a military self-defense and fighting system developed for the Israel Defense Forces. I found it to be efficient and easy to remember and the more I practiced and trained, the more empowered I felt.

Over time I began to find Nicole again. There were parts of me from the past that remained but there was no going back to being the naïve, trusting and carefree girl that I used to be. I had experienced too much pain and survived to much darkness to be that person again. Rediscovering yourself again is a process. It takes time, trial and error and being open to meeting new people and trying new experiences.

CHAPTER 31

Healing through Helping

It took me two years after leaving my abuser to finally begin talking about my experiences with anyone outside of my close circle. As I continued to heal and gain strength, I found myself sharing more with others, posting more on those Domestic Violence related social media sites and counseling new victims that reached out to me asking questions or who needed help on those sites.

In time I realized that I had nothing to be ashamed of or embarrassed about as I did nothing wrong to make my abuser abuse me. He was the one who was flawed, he was the one that should feel embarrassed and ashamed of his behavior. I also became more aware of how much victim shaming and blaming our society does through the media, jokes, victim blaming comments about domestic violence situations and the way the media often reports cases of domestic violence and related homicides.

Once my ex-husband was finally incarcerated, I felt that it was time for me to speak up and share my story in hopes of educating people on the realities of domestic violence and that it is not as easy as "just leaving" which is the advice given to so many victims. I began with telling my story on my own Facebook page and on other Social Media outlets where victims still living in fear might read it. I then teamed up with Break the Silence for my first event at Eastern Michigan University and from there things began to take on a life of their own.

I began being asked to speak to clubs and organizations, to sororities and youth groups. Over time, schools, police organizations and domestic violence shelters invited me to speak. As I became more known in the community for my advocacy work, the more victims or victim's family members began reaching out to me for help and I began meeting with them for lunch, coffee, dinner or just speaking to them over the phone if they lived too far away.

I began to realize that the more I raised awareness, the more I helped others and the more I spoke up the better I felt about myself and the person that I was becoming. Advocating for others has been a large part of my healing journey. I have come to understand, that for me because I was able to escape and survive my abusive relationship it is incredibly important to me to try and help others survive by giving them the hope and tools to escape. I also have become passionate about domestic violence prevention and began presenting information about red flags and warning signs to young adults so they never have to experience an abusive relationship at all.

I also knew in my heart of hearts that I would not be able to do this work any longer once my ex-husband was released from prison and that drove me to do as much as possible with the short amount of time that I had been gifted.

It is amazing how far I have come from being a woman that was not comfortable making eye contact with others and being terrified of public speaking when I was in an abusive relationship to being a woman who can now speak in front of 3,000 people without fear.

CHAPTER 32

The Unexpected Gift

By November 2016, it had been well over two years since I had been contacted by law enforcement related to my ex-husband for any reason. I had faithfully been attending his yearly parole hearings and pleading with the board to keep him incarcerated for as long as possible but his maximum sentencing date was approaching and I knew I had to start planning where the boys and I were going to relocate before his release.

I remember vividly that I was sitting in my coworker's office that cold November day assisting her with some client resources when I unexpectedly received a call from a detective from the Michigan State Police post in Ste St Marie which is in the Upper Peninsula of Michigan. "Ms. Beverly" he began", "Do you know any inmates housed at the Newbury Correction Facility?" It took me a minute to make the connection to what he was saying. "Yes", I replied, "I believe that is where my ex-husband is currently incarcerated." The detective replied, "I am obligated to inform you that there is an inmate currently serving time with your ex-husband at the Newbury facility who has come forward stating that your ex-husband has offered him $5,000 to kill you and possibly your children."

I am quite sure that the Detective calling me was not expecting the reaction that he received from me but for the first time in years a trickle of hope coursed through my veins and I could not hide it. "Really?" I replied with cautious excitement, "Is he willing to testify to this?" The detective shared that the other inmate was willing to wear a wire and was willing to testify against my ex-husband in court.

"Is he asking for a deal if he testifies or some type of early release?" I asked, not wanting to get my hopes up again. "No", replied the detective, "He stated that he is not asking for any type of deal. He has shared that he is very concerned about your safety and your children's safety and he wants to do the right thing."

I then asked the detective if he was aware of the previous attempts to hire that had not been prosecuted in Wayne and Washtenaw Counties. He stated that he was not and that he was not aware of any type of alert or communication system in place between the State Police Posts or between the State Police and the prisons that would have alerted him to the previous investigations or inmate statements. Again, I was absolutely stunned and left wondering how this was possible considering the technology that is available today. Shocked at how this lack of communication and documentation was incredibly dangerous and putting people's lives at risk. Appalled because my ex-husband had attempted to hire multiple people to kill me and there was absolutely no paper trail connecting the dots.

"So, what happens next?" I asked. The detective instructed me to forward him the information and reports from the previous investigations. Thankfully I had saved all records of them. I also offered to connect him with the Washtenaw County Prosecutor who had been my biggest advocate over the past few years, Anna Slawson. He accepted the offer and stated, "the next steps are for me to review what you are sending me, talk to Prosecutor Slawson and to start a full investigation here at Newbury including getting a wired recording of your ex-husband soliciting for your murder."

Despite all of the previous times I had been disappointed by the legal system, hope was beginning to flow through me again. I could feel it growing and for the first time in a long time I felt my fighting spirit begin to return. I immediately contacted Washtenaw County Prosecutor Anna Slawson and she sent this email to Detective Schmitd that same day.

(Email from Anna Slawson APA)

November 15, 2016

Detective Schmitd,

I have recently been advised by Nicole Beverly that her ex-husband has reprised his role as solicitor. He has a very long history regarding this behavior. Based on my knowledge of his Washtenaw County offenses and attempted offense, I consider Mr. Beverly one of our most dangerous and lethal threats returning back to our community. I know Mr. Beverly is awaiting information regarding his Parole acceptance/denial and that could come at any hour. I know that you are off for a few days and I do not want your investigation to be hampered by the Parole Board granting release then retracting the decision after your return. I have asked our local MSP go to guy, Sgt. Singleton to reach out to you to confirm that MSP has notified the Parole Board about a pending investigation and to get next steps.

The Office of the Prosecuting Attorney of Washtenaw County will provide any information that we have retained that may assist in your current investigation. I have copied Detective Mike Boyd from the Washtenaw County Sheriff's Department, he was the OIC in past Beverly investigations. I have also copied Stephanie King, Victim Advocate from our office who is also a wealth of information regarding all things Kevin Beverly.

—Anna Slawson

Excerpt from Police Report #089-0002095-16

Date: 11/10/2016 #089-0002095-16

SOLICITATION TO COMMIT MURDER

I was contacted on 11/10/16 by Inspector Rothchild at the Newberry Correctional Facility (NCF) in reference to a possible Solicitation to Commit Murder case. The had information from an officer that was contacted by an inmate, advising that his cell mate was asking him how much it would cost to harm his ex-wife. My investigation began at this time.

Inspector Rothchild advised that back on 11/09/16 he spoke with inmate Lopez who said he had 3-4 separate conversations with prisoner BEVERLY regarding his wanting his ex-wife hurt. Inmate Lopez was not sure if BEVERLY was still married or divorced. He reported the first conversation was sometime around April 2016. He said that they also discussed a monetary amount of $5,000 and BEVERLY wanted to know if that would be enough to hurt his ex-wife. Lopez also advised that at this time BEVERLY spoke of an alibi for himself while the criminal act occurred.

Lopez stated that approximately twice per week for the last several months he has heard BEVERLY mutter words such as "bitch" and "whore" as he walked around his cube. Lopez stated that BEVERLY was not talking to anybody in general, but just muttering those words to himself. It is Lopez's belief that he (BEVERLY) was muttering about his ex-wife. At this time Lopez also stated that he was willing to cooperate with the State Police to investigate this matter and would also be willing to wear an electronic device to record any conversations.

Inspector Rothchild advised that inmate BEVERLY had recently had a parole board hearing and they were awaiting a decision on his parole as his earliest out date has since past in 2014 and his latest out date is 10/17.

Interview with inmate Ramone Lopez:

I met with the NCF Inspectors on 11/28/16 at approximately 8:30 am. They had inmate Lopez come into the room also to speak with me. I advised inmate Lopez that he was not in trouble and it was my understanding he was here on his own accord to assist in this investigation. Inmate Lopez agreed to assist me in this investigation. I advised Lopez that I had spoken with the inspector and I understood he had information from one of his cell mates and asked if he would like to talk to me about that and he advised me that he would.

Inmate Lopez advised that he is originally from the Lansing area. He stated that this was his first time in prison. He said that he resides in the "D" cube, bunk 12. He advised that he first started hearing his cell mate, KEVIN BEVERLY (a/k/a "The Green Mile"), talk about his ex-wife back in February or March of this year. He said that BEVERLY was angry with his ex-wife. He said that BEVERLY had inquired "What can you get for $5,000? Could you get somebody to hurt somebody?". He said that on another occasion BEVERLY had stated to inmate Lopez "Remember what we were talking about?'. BEVERLY then inquired of Lopez when he was due to get out of prison. BEVERLY discussed the idea of killing his ex-wife with a lethal heroin overdose. He then made the comment, "I can't wait to get that fucking cunt".

Inmate Lopez advised that there were other conversations about inmate BEVERLY inquiring about having something done to his ex-wife and possibly his children also. He advised that another inmate mentioned knowing something about this and referred to him as Mr. Bill". He stated that Mr. Bill has made comments to inmate Lopez that "The Green Mile has problems. He's going to get out and kill that bitch. If he's talking about that kind of stuff when he's sober, what do you think is going to happen after a few drinks?"

CHAPTER 33

The Longest Wait

From the date of that first call from Detective Schmitd on November 12, 2016, I waited as patiently as I could for updates and news on what was happening with the investigation. I documented every phone call, conversation and email sent as I had learned to do over the past 6 years to keep details straight and have a paper trail of events for myself.

I forwarded all previous police reports and documentation that I had to Detective Schmitd. I also contacted the Parole Board multiple times from November 12th through December 5th to make them aware of the current investigation and sent them the same information plus case updates about the current investigation in hopes that they would hold off on their decision about Parole during the investigation as it could impact how my ex-husband would respond. If he knew he was being released soon he may not keep talking about his desire to hire someone to kill me and it could directly effect whether or not enough information could finally be obtained for new charges this time.

On December 13, 2016 I heard back from Detective Schmitd and he reported that they had not yet attempted the wire because they were waiting for the Parole board to send a letter denying parole. Since that had not happened, he planned to go back to Newberry Prison and attempt the wire next week. He stated that the inmate was still willing to cooperate and is asking for nothing in return for wearing the wire or testifying if necessary because he is so concerned about something happening to our family.

The final thing he stated during the conversation was that he had talked to Jeron Whitfield, Supervisor at the Michigan Parole Department about all of the new information and was told that unless there were new charges issued the plan was still to release my ex-husband in June. That meant that unless this investigation was successful, I had six months until my ex-husband was released from prison. I felt physically ill just hearing those words.

On December 16, 2016 I received a letter from the Michigan State Parole Board that stated that after careful consideration, the parole board had voted to grant parole to the prisoner (My ex-husband).

The letter went on to state that his release was tentatively scheduled to occur on or about 6/8/2017. The letter further stated that "Reasonable assurance exists that the prisoner will not become a menace to society or to the public safety." The letter and notice of decision further stated that, "the Prisoner expresses remorse, has satisfactory block reports, interacts well with staff/prisoners and has a positive attitude about challenges ahead."

This of course was an absolute shock to my system because what I was reading was not making an ounce of sense to me! This same Parole Board saying my ex-husband was not a threat had the information about the current investigation for attempt to hire for murder, all of the information and police reports about his multiple attempts to hire people to kill me in the past, the statements from other inmates stating that he was planning to kill myself and my children upon release and all of the reports of his multiple incidents of prison misconduct including fights on "12/30/12, 3/22/16, 3/24/16, Infractions for Being Out of Place on 11/10/15, 3/21/16 and infractions for Interference With The Administration Of Rules on 1/2/15, 4/2/15, 9/20/16."

I was trying hard to understand how this could even be possible. How could a system be this flawed when people's lives were on the line? They were going to release a man intent on killing his family just days before our oldest son was set to graduate from High School.

CHAPTER 34

The Wait Goes On

On January 3, 2017, I was contacted by Detective Schmitd indicating that they had finally located the notice of motion for full legal custody and permission to leave the state that I had sent certified mail to the prison several weeks earlier. He shared that they planned to wire the cooperating inmate within the next day or two and that he would contact me when he had more information. I remember feeling helpless and I could feel the clocking ticking down the minutes until June.

One week later, on January 10, 2017 I received a call back from Detective Schmitd indicating that the wire has not been successful as my ex-husband has been very quiet since receiving the letter from the Parole Department approving his Parole in June. He also mentioned that the letters from the inmates written at Jackson Prison regarding my ex-husband's plans to kill us were not found anywhere in Kevin's prison files. I told him that I would attempt to locate them and send them to him as quickly as possible.

On January 12, 2017, I was having difficulty locating my copies of the letters from Jackson Prison. I had previously provided the letters to the Parole Board for parole consideration, so I contacted them and requested that they send the letters over to Detective Schmitd related to the current investigation. The woman that I spoke with at the Parole Board informed me that they were not allowed release the letters to me or Detective Schmitd even though I was the one that had provided them the letters in the first place. This obviously made no sense to me and I was absolutely furious but instead of wasting any more time trying to argue my point, I made the decision to head straight to the Washtenaw County Court House where I knew that there were copies of the letters in my recent court records. I paid $25 to have the copies made and emailed them to Detective Schmitd immediately.

From January 19, 2017- January 29, 2017, I left three messages for Detective Schmitd to call me back with any updates, as I knew my ex-husband would have received the notice that I had mailed informing him that my motion to obtain full legal custody and move out of the State had been granted by the court.

Three more weeks had gone by and on February 1st, 2017 Detective Schmitd finally answered his phone and indicated that there had been some developments and that the inmate wearing the wire felt that he had gotten some good evidence on recording of Kevin talking about setting up my murder. The inmate requested to wear the wire one more time in an attempt to get more evidence. He further explained that he had to get the device from the inmate and download the current recording then get it back to the inmate so that he could attempt to wear it one more time.

Detective Schmidt stated that he would let me know when he was certain that he had enough evidence to present the case to Newbury Prosecutor Jonathan Freeman. He suggested that I write a letter to Mr. Freeman as well explaining how all of this has affected my life and the lives of my children. Detective Schmitd also noted that if Prosecutor Freeman denied prosecution, he could still go to the Attorney General for a second opinion as he had done on other cases. I thought it was unusual that he was already talking about the possibility of Prosecutor Freeman denying the case especially due to the severity, but I didn't dwell on that statement.

From February 6, 2017- February 15, 2017, I left Detective Schmitd three voicemail messages and one email asking him to please provide me updates as I was feeling incredibly anxious and worried and the clock was ticking very quickly towards my ex-husbands parole date. I was still holding on to so much hope feeling there was no way he could possibly get away with this crime again. I tried my best to focus on work and my kids, but it was becoming increasingly difficult.

On February 16, 2017 I called Detective Schmitd again and he answered the call. He stated that his mother had passed away and he had been out of town for the past two weeks. He then shared that the audio recording obtained from the first wire attempt was difficult to hear due to background noise as there was a football game on TV at the time of the conversation. The detective noted that he had sent his audio team a copy of the recording to see if they could clean it up. He added that the inmate had requested to wear the wire again but that he was unaware as to whether or not that had happened since he had just gotten back into town and the prison inspector had been out sick this week.

After this conversation, it dawned on me that it had been three months since the first phone call I had received about this new threat on my life and essentially nothing had happened in terms of forward movement. It was becoming clear to me that this case was not a priority or maybe this small State Police Department was out of their league.

I could feel the world beginning to close in on me and it was becoming harder and harder to function at work and harder and harder to get out of bed. Because this was an open investigation, and we did not want word getting out about it to anyone the only people I could really talk to about this were my Mother and Sister. To the rest of the world I had to pretend like this horrible situation was not occurring. Another two weeks went by with no communication from Detective Schmitd.

On March 1, 2017 I called Detective Schmitd for an update because I had heard nothing from anyone about the investigation and he stated that he was still waiting for the audio department to "clean up" the recording obtained several weeks ago. He said that the plan was for the other inmate to still attempt to get another audio recording that was clearer and that he would call me as soon as he had any updated information.

Letter to Luce County Prosecutor Jonathan Freeman

February 9, 2017

Dear Mr. Freeman,

My name is Nicole Beverly and I understand that you are the Prosecutor that is reviewing the investigation/case involving my ex-husband Kevin Beverly and his attempt to solicit for my murder. I asked Detective Schmitd for your contact information so that I could have the opportunity to share my fears and concerns related to my ex-husband and his continued attempts to solicit inmates for my murder and the murder of my children.

Prior to his incarceration Mr. Beverly was both physically and emotionally abusive towards me. He once held his gun to my head and told me all of the reasons that he should kill me. Mr. Beverly would often tell me that if I told anyone about his abuse or if I left him he would hunt me down like a dog no matter how far I went or how hard I tried to hide from him. He said that once he found me he would take me by surprise and would slit my throat, shoot me, torture me, disfigure me, paralyze me, etc… After I finally got up the courage to leave the marriage due to his abuse he began to stalk and threaten to kill me despite a personal protection order and his probation requirements. As a result of his behavior he had several probation and personal protection violations prior to his most recent incarceration for aggravated stalking. Through his words and actions over the past 6 years Mr. Beverly has made it clear that he intends to kill me and possibly my children upon his release from prison and has attempted to others to kill myself and my children for him.

As I am sure you are aware since his incarceration began in 2012 for aggravated stalking there have been three previous inmates that have come forward stating that my ex-husband Kevin Beverly approached them with detailed offers to kill me for money with no resulting charges. The first attempt to hire was not criminally charged in Washtenaw County because although the inmate that came forward had passed a polygraph exam related to the allegations, the County would not make any deals with the inmate and he refused to testify.

The second attempt to hire occurred at the Detroit Re-entry Center where two inmates came forward stating that Mr. Beverly had inquired about paying them for my murder and the murder of my children. Those gentleman had agreed to wear a wire to obtain evidence for the Wayne County State Police when there was a huge lack of communication between the parole board, Jackson Prison and the Michigan State Police that resulted in Mr. Beverly being returned to Jackson Prison before the two inmates that had agreed to wear a wire to gather evidence were able to obtain any recorded solicitation attempts therefore no new charges were issued for a second time.

It should be noted that there were also two other inmates at Jackson Prison that had come forward with written statements in 2013 stating that Mr. Beverly was regularly stating that as soon as he was released from prison he planned to find me, kill my children in front of me, then torture me to death. It is unbelievable to most that not including this most recent investigation at Newberry Prison, 5 separate inmates from three different facilities reporting very similar information and attempting to prevent something horrible from happening to myself and my children with no new charges resulting!

Unfortunately, I have become accustomed to living my life looking over my shoulder due to Mr. Beverly's repeated threats to kill me and to solicit for my murder. It is incredibly unfair to both myself and my amazing children to have to live our lives this way. I have become conditioned to always being aware of my surroundings, knowing where exits are, never sitting with my back to a door, triple checking locks and alarms, setting up passwords and lock down procedures at my work and my children's school and never being able to trust the intentions of unfamiliar people. It is incredibly disappointing to me that despite a clear pattern of behavior no new charges have been filed against Mr. Beverly up until this point. I am terrified of Mr. Beverly being released from prison as it is clear that his intent is to kill me and possibly my children. I am struggling with the decision to give up everything I have in order to protect myself and my children. It is a decision that no one should be forced to make.

If Mr. Beverly does not face new charges I am faced with the choice of either giving up my amazing job, selling my home, pulling my children out of their neighborhood and school where they are excelling and leaving behind our family and friends or stay and live in fear as it is clear based on his behavior and statements that he plans to kill me or have me killed once he is released from prison in July. It is a decision that is causing me intense anxiety and stress on a daily basis.

Despite all of this I am remaining hopeful that new charges will be filed against Mr. Beverly as a result of this current investigation and that he will be kept behind bars where he cannot harm myself or my children. No one should be given this many chances to attempt to solicit for someone's murder without consequences.

If you have any questions for me or would like to meet with me in person or via Skype I would be happy to do so. Washtenaw County Prosecutor Anna Slawson would also be happy to speak with you and provide you with more information as well.

Thank you for your time and consideration.

Sincerely,

Nicole Beverly

CHAPTER 35

Planning for the Worst

On March 27, 2017 Ann Arbor Prosecutor Anna Slawson and victim advocate Stephanie King reached out to me about setting up a Safety Planning Meeting for our family as there had still not been new charges issued against my ex-husband and it was very possible that he would be getting out within the next three months. We scheduled the meeting for April 6, 2017 and Stephanie said that she would email me a copy of the agenda as soon as she had it.

On April 1, 2017, I received a phone call from Anna Slawson that she wanted to talk to me about the Safety Planning Meeting Agenda before the victim advocate emailed it to me. I could tell that she was speaking slowly and carefully choosing her words.

She went on to apologize for the need to have this conversation and went on to explain that the reason that she wanted to talk to me personally was that some of the items on the agenda were very difficult to discuss but that because of the high lethality that we faced once my ex-husband was released they were necessary.

She paused and shared that the Sheriff's Department was requesting biological samples from myself and the boys.

I was confused. Biological Samples I asked? She apologized again for even having to have this discussion with me but she felt that she was the best person to have it with me since she has been involved with our case for so long. She paused and went on to say, "We are requesting all of your dental records, fingerprints, recent pictures and pictures of any tattoos of you and the boys."

It took a few seconds to register what she was saying to me but when it did, I literally felt as though someone had just punched me in the gut with full force.

They were requesting ways that they would be able to identify our bodies when he killed us. They knew he was going to kill us and there was no one with the power to help us stepping up and doing it. I could not catch my breath and was unable to speak until the wave of deep emotion calmed.

Prosecutor Slawson again expressed her apologies and added that they would need to send the SWAT team to my house to map it in case of emergency or hostage situation and that they would be creating school safety plans with both of my son's schools. She stated that my house would also be flagged by dispatch as a high priority location as well as any calls coming in from my cell phone or those of my children.

I never in my life imagined that I'd ever be asked to provide the police with ways to identify my body or the bodies of my children, but this was now my reality and it was absolutely horrible. Just a few months ago I had so much hope that new charges would be filed and there would be no possible way that he would be released and allowed to torment us again. That hope was fading fast.

On April 6, 2017 my mother and sister attended my safety planning meeting with me. Around the table sat multiple Sheriff's Deputies, Lincoln School Liaisons, Prosecutors, Parole Officers and Victim Advocates that had been invited by Prosecutor Slawson. We again discussed my ex-husband's impending release and the extremely high lethality risk that my children and I would be facing either from my ex-husband or someone that he might try to hire to kill us.

We discussed the need for the SWAT team to map my house, the need for our dental records and fingerprints along with updated safety plans for my job, my youngest son's school and at Delaware State University where my oldest son would soon be heading to college. It was also decided that my house would be clearly flagged for dispatch as a priority response home due to the risk of lethality.

During the meeting the Washtenaw Prosecutor's office offered to pay for a special GPS monitor for me to wear if my ex-husband violated his tether conditions and came into our county and triggered his tether. The GPS monitor would immediately notify me that he had entered the county. The Parole Department said that they could not allow this because it was "against protocol."

Instead the current protocol would be in place which consisted of the tether company calling the parole officer if a tether monitor went off, then it would be up to the parole officer to contact the police and either the police or the parole officer could contact me to give me a warning if they felt it was necessary.

I recall sitting there frustrated and angry asking them what happens if the parole officer is in a meeting or asleep when the company calls? What if no one calls me to warn me? None of my concerns mattered to the Parole Department at that moment because it was "against protocol".

CHAPTER 36

Devastation

On April 17, 2017, an entire five months after I had received the initial phone call about the inmate coming forward in Luce County with information about my ex-husband again attempting to hire someone to murder me, I received another phone call from Detective Schmitd. He was calling to notify me that he had still not gotten any new information from Newberry Prison and that he "assumed" that meant they did not have any new recorded evidence.

Detective Schmitd also calmly stated that Prosecutor Freeman was refusing to move forward with charges against my ex-husband with the current evidence despite the Luce County inmate being willing to testify, take a polygraph exam as well as my ex-husband's previous attempts to hire inmates in three other counties to kill me. He noted that he had forwarded all of his reports to the Attorney General's office for their consideration to prosecute despite Prosecutor Freeman's refusal to move forward with new charges.

I sat at my desk for a long time, numb from the shock and disappointment. I could not believe that the system was letting me down again and refusing to protect my family from this man who was dead set on killing us. A man who the police and prosecutors and everyone else at that safety planning meeting knew was very likely going to kill us once he was released from prison in just two short months.

CHAPTER 37

Fight or Flight

After receiving the news that the Luce County Prosecutor adamantly refused to move forward with new charges against my ex-husband, I attempted to contact him by phone and email several times from May 5, 2017 through May 11, 2017 and he refused to talk to me. Prosecutor Freeman's assistant Lana told me that she was instructed to be the one to communicate with me. I remember breaking into tears while on the phone with her telling her that I just wanted him to explain to me why he was not willing to at least attempt to try the case considering the documented history of attempts to hire for murder in the other counties.

I desperately needed to understand why no one was helping my family yet again. I asked Lana what my rights were at this point as a victim and she stated that "she did not know" and would "ask John to call me." Shockingly, he never did.

In my heart of hearts, I believed that my ex-husband was finally going to face new charges in Luce County. We had the whole package, a witness willing to testify, willing to take a polygraph and wear a wire to get recorded evidence. There was another inmate that was willing to testify to hearing my ex-husband make similar statements and neither of them was asking for a deal. What more did we need?

I was certain that we would finally have new charges against my ex-husband that would keep him in prison and protect my family for a much longer time. To say I was shocked and devastated to learn that the Prosecutor was refusing to move forward with the case would be an understatement. The fact that my ex-husband would be released from prison in just two short months despite everything he had done absolutely devastated me.

There were times that I cried so hard that I vomited. Days that I had to physically force myself out of bed. Nights when I would fall down on my knees and pray that someone somewhere would finally step in and help us. I could not understand how it was even possible that the people that were in hired positions to protect us were failing us again.

I would often think about all of the inmates who had taken chances coming forward to help us. They were the ones who had risked their own safety by coming forward for nothing to be done time and time again. I was so grateful to them for at least trying to do the right thing.

I found myself vacillating between so many different emotions every single day and I was doing my best to hide my emotions from my own children and to function at work with my coworkers and the children that I worked with every day so they wouldn't see my pain and fear showing through.

I learned to cry in the bathroom or after my kids had gone to sleep. I also realized that the skill of turning my emotions on and off that I had learned as a survival skill after years of living with an abuser came in very handy during this difficult time. It was especially helpful when I still had to get up and function every day as a parent, social worker and an advocate for other victims.

Somehow, I gathered the strength to pick myself up off of the floor and I started making phone calls to domestic violence agencies across the State of Michigan for help with my situation. Our local shelter referred me to the State Coalition Against Domestic Violence who told me they did not provide direct services to victims and that there was nothing they could do to help me. They then referred me right back to my local shelter.

I spent hours contacting countless women's resource centers, domestic violence agencies and legal resource agencies only to be told time and time again that they could not help me. It honestly felt like a huge circle of disappointment where I kept being referred back to whatever agency I had last called or called the day before.

Through those hours spent making phone calls I learned that there was no designated relocation funding for victims of domestic violence and stalking in the State of Michigan. There were also no Domestic Violence agencies that offered this assistance in our State aside from one organization, The Angel House that paid for a plane or bus ticket for you to leave the state to head directly to a shelter for further resources and help.

There were no agencies nearby to help me with the process of name and social security number changes, there is no address confidentiality program in Michigan to protect the addresses of victims from their abusers as there is in many other states. The more phone calls that I made, the more apparent it became that no one really seemed to be aware or concerned about this huge problem.

I was referred by a fellow survivor to an expert in Washington DC who was very direct in telling me that if I relocated and only changed my name my ex-husband would still be able to hire a private investigator and find me within a ten-minute search using my social security number. She went on to explain that if I also changed my Social Security Number, I would lose all of my work history, my college degrees and and established credit because I would essentially be a new person starting over again with nothing.

I was shocked because this thought had never even crossed my mind before. She let me know that this was one of the leading causes of homelessness in domestic violence victims that have to take such measures to protect themselves and I remember feeling utterly hopeless yet infuriated at the same time.

Because of my income as a clinical social worker I made too much money on paper to obtain any legal assistance to file for full legal custody of my boys, to file for permission to move them out of the State or to help with all of the legal paperwork necessary for our name and social security number changes.

Because of my modest income I fell in that gap area of not qualifying for legal assistance and not being able to afford an attorney myself. That meant I had to take things into my own hands. I read up on the topics, filed the paperwork and represented myself in court while hoping for the best.

While I was doing the work to prepare the motions for full custody and to relocate out of State, I began to experience a very deep internal struggle. Trying to decide whether it was worth it to try and fight to get the legal system to help me keep my ex-husband behind bars or to just put all of my time and energy outside of work into preparing to disappear from the state. I continued to talk to my friends and family about it, I talked to a therapist about it, I went to a psychic, I wrote out lists of pros and cons and in the end I decided that I owed it to myself and my children to do both.

As a last-ditch effort, I began calling attorneys to see if any of them would be willing to represent me if I were to sue the State of Michigan for Failure to Protect as a few different survivors in other states had suggested that I do. I was immediately turned down by all of the larger legal firm's people had advised me to call. The largest firms in our area all told me that there was not enough money to be made with my case. After at least a dozen calls I finally found an attorney that sat down and met with me and we began to discuss strategy and cost versus the benefit of me staying and fighting the legal system.

CHAPTER 38

Yet Another Set Back

On May 4, 2017, Detective Schmitd called me to let me know that he had spoken to the Attorney General's office and they were unable to find the paperwork he sent over to them asking for help with my case.

On May 5, 2017, Detective Schmitd called me back to let me know that he had received a phone call from one of the Division Chiefs indicating that the package had been found and that the person who normally assigns new cases was out on maternity leave so it had been misplaced. The Division Chief added that he did review the file himself and was denying the case and referring it back to the Luce County Prosecutor Jonathan Freeman. The Division Chief offered no explanation other than it was Luce County's decision.

On May 9, 2017, I called the Attorney General's office to get information as to why they had so quickly denied my case and was transferred to the department of the Division Chief who had done the review of my case. A woman named Mary answered the phone and when I explained to her why I was calling she was so incredibly rude, condescending and cruel to me that I immediately burst into tears which is something that has rarely happened to me. The combination of her cruelness and the immense weight on my shoulders was just too much for me to bear.

She went on coldly to tell me that I should not be calling them and that I needed to call the Michigan Department of Corrections if I had any questions. Mary refused to even listen to what I was trying to ask her and she dismissed my call by stating there was nothing else the Attorney General's office could do to help.

I sat alone in my living room sobbing and feeling so angry, terrified and hopeless that I was having trouble catching my breath. I could not believe I was being treated this way. I was a victim begging for help and no matter where I turned no one was willing to help me or my children.

CHAPTER 39

Desperate Measures

Between May 11, 2017 and May 22, 2017, I sent emails and left voicemails for any and every one that I could think of who might have the power to help me. The Governor, The Lieutenant Governor, My State Representatives, Senators and Congresswomen, The Attorney General, The State Victim Advocate, The Director of the Michigan Domestic Violence and Sexual Assault Coalition, The Director of The National Coalition for Domestic Violence, The Crime Victims

Services Commission and every Domestic Violence Organization within 100 miles of me.

After making all of these phone calls and sending all of these emails describing my family's situation, I heard back from two people. TWO.

On May 19, 2017 I received a phone call from a Victim Advocate at the Attorney General's office. He let me know that there were no victim relocation funds in the State of Michigan but that he would contact some resources and get back with me. He told me however to, "not get my hopes up".

On May 19, 2017 I received a phone call from a representative at the Michigan Department of Corrections Legislative Office. He let me know that he had been asked to contact me by the Lieutenant Governor's office. He was very patient with me as I explained to him what was happening and how the parole board had jeopardized the outcome of an open investigation and how they were still planning to release him in June, just a few weeks from now.

I explained my fears and that my oldest son would not have even graduated before the date set for my ex-husband's release. The representative indicated that he would contact the parole board and request that parole be pushed back.

On May 30th, 2017 I received a l letter from the Parole Board indicating that they had pushed my ex-husband's release back by one month. One month... This would at least get us through Myles graduation.

CHAPTER 40

The Shed

On May 17, 2017, just weeks after our Safety Planning meeting my boys and I were at home together. At approximately 10 pm my dog Sapphire began acting very strangely. She was being very clingy with us, crying but not barking like she normally would if she needed to go outside.

At about 10:05 pm, I finally got up to make her go outside and I noticed that the interior light of the shed in my backyard was turned on. This was unusual for several reasons. One, you can only turn the shed light on from inside of the shed using the circuit breaker that is inside. Two, I knew I had not been out in the shed in the past several days. Three, my boys never went inside the shed unless I had asked them to and I had not. Just to be sure I asked them both if they had been out there the night before or that morning for any reason and they both indicated that they had not.

Under normal circumstances, a person who isn't aware that multiple people have been offered money to kill them would probably just walk out to that shed to turn out the light. Because I knew there had been multiple attempts by my ex-husband to do that and he only had a few weeks left of an alibi there was no way in hell I was going outside to turn that shed light out.

I told the boys that we were locking down the house and closing all of the blinds. I put my firearm on my hip and stayed alert but did not overreact because I did not want my kids to be more fearful than they already were.

At 10:35 my youngest son, Carter yelled into the next room to tell me that the shed light had just been turned off. Again, we know that the light can only be turned on and off from inside of the shed. He was visibly upset and shaken so I told him that I was going to call the police and have them come out to check the shed and make sure that everything was okay.

As I was calling 911, I let my son know that I had just had a meeting with the police and that our house was on a special list to be responded to more quickly than other houses because of the past issues with his Dad.

At 10:37 pm I called 911 and explained to the Washtenaw County Sheriff Department dispatcher that our house was flagged as high priority due to my ex-husband attempting to hire people to kill me from prison and that he had a history of aggravated stalking. I told her how the shed light had been turned on and off by someone from inside of the shed.

At 11:33 pm the police had still not responded to our house. My kids were extremely upset and afraid and while I was trying to reassure them that everything was going to be okay, I was feeling the same fear.

At 11:34 pm I called 911 again and asked if my house was still flagged as a priority because no one had yet responded to my call. The dispatcher responded that yes, she saw that our house was flagged but that officers were still busy out on other calls and that someone was on their way now. I made the decision to document everything that was happening on Facebook so that other people would be aware of what was happening should something happen to us before an officer arrived on the scene.

At 11:45 pm a Deputy finally responded, and I again explained the situation from beginning to end. He went outside to the shed, opened the door and looked around with a flashlight. Then he asked me to come outside to see if anything was missing and it was not. He suggested that I get a better lock for the shed and stated that he would write up a report for the incident. When I asked him why it took him an hour and 10 minutes to respond when our house was supposed to be flagged as high priority, he stated that they were short officers and they were all out on other calls.

That night my son Carter, then 13 years old, placed a kitchen knife next to his sleeping brother Myles who was then 17 years old. He then locked and duct-taped his door shut and slept with a screwdriver next to him in bed in an attempt to stay safe.

Seeing that absolutely broke my heart and made me realize that even with a safety plan created by the most powerful people in my county it was not going to be enough to protect us from my ex-husband, especially once he was released from prison.

The next morning the low tire pressure light was on in my car and I took it in immediately to get a hole patched that was causing the leak. It was just another sign that we weren't safe, and my weariness grew even greater.

CHAPTER 41

The GoFundMe

On May 23, 2017 at 9:00 pm my friend and fellow domestic violence survivor Amy Donalds launched a GoFundMe for relocation funds for myself and my children. We knew it would be necessary for moving expenses, a rental deposit, rent, etc... it would be very difficult for me until I could find a job making anywhere near what I was making in my current career.

In the GoFundMe description, we included the history of abuse, stalking, attempts to hire for my murder and direct statements from police reports so people would understand the seriousness and urgency of our situation.

I was amazed at how quickly people began donating, sharing and expressing their outrage at my family's situation. They were having a hard time understanding how the system could possibly have let us down so many times and why no one was protecting us.

People from across the nation began offering us safe places to stay, gas cards and free rent. It was so incredibly moving to see and feel how much people who did not even know us cared and wanted to keep my family safe. People began asking what else they could do to help so we posted information on how to contact the Attorney General's Office and request that they take our case and protect my family. People began to contact the Attorney General's office in droves.

Kristen Jordan Shamus, writer for the Detroit Free Press reached out to me for more information about my story. After hearing the details she wanted to tell my story and get my family as much support as possible.

Kristen and I spent several days doing interviews and going over dates and case details. Because my case spanned so many years and has so many details it is difficult even for me to tell it in a concise manner, but Kristen somehow pulled it off and told my story in a very powerful way.

CHAPTER 42

Front Page News

On Sunday, July 3rd, 2017 The Detroit Free Press ran our story front page in a two and half page spread. They also included a video interview of me talking about our case on the online version of our story.

Kristen not only shared our story, she also shared ways that people could help us by including information about our GoFundMe and the fact that our last hope was the Attorney General's Office. Within the next 24 hours our story began to go viral hitting news outlets across the county.

After so many years of feeling like no one cared about what happened to us, it was absolutely amazing to experience the immense amount of support that we were receiving from people across the nation. We went from $5,000 in donations to $15,000 in donations in just a few days and those who could not contribute financially were offering us places to stay or were contacting the Attorney General's office to advocate for us and keep us safe.

The weekend of July 7, 2017 I held a moving sale at my home in an attempt to get more relocation funds together and get rid of belongings that I knew we would not be able to move across the country with us.

The GoFundMe continued to get viral support. This was a huge relief to me as I knew we would be struggling after we moved. I knew how hard it was going to be for me to get employment once my name and social security number were officially changed.

I had already met with an attorney at the University of Michigan Law School who was willing to help me make those changes.

The week of July 10th I began having home repairs done in preparation for selling our home as we were being forced to relocate. That same week, Tom Walker, a local real estate agent reached out to me and offered to sell our home without his receiving any commission. Again, I was taken aback by the generosity and kindness of people.

I had already been exploring relocation locations and had decided on a destination, so I began researching rentals in that area. A problem arose related to my renting an apartment or house because I had not yet changed my name legally. This meant I would need someone else not well known to my abuser to be willing put a rental in their name so my ex-husband could not find me. There was also a good chance that I would still need to do that even after my name change as I would then have no employment or credit history. I began inquiring about paying a full year's lease upfront and most rental owners seemed suspicious about my request.

On July 9th, 2017, I received a second phone call from the Attorney General's Victim Advocate asking me to come in for a meeting with a few members of their team to discuss my case on July 12th, 2017. We set a time for 2:00 pm and I began to gather all of my documentation so that I could make the most powerful impression possible in that meeting. I was afraid to get my hopes up again because they had been squashed so many times before and I knew that this would be my only chance to convince them to take our case.

CHAPTER 43

Things Take a Turn

On July 12th, 2017 at 2:00 pm, I walked into the Cadillac Building in Detroit, Michigan filled with anticipation and determination. The Victim Advocate that I had been speaking with met me at the building entrance and escorted me up the elevators to The Attorney General's Office. Once in the elevator he let me know that the meeting was going to be a bit larger than he had anticipated. At that point, all I could do was nod and say okay because I knew this was my last opportunity to get the help I desperately needed.

As we entered the room, I was very surprised to see a large conference table filled with people. I took the open seat in the middle of them all as he went around the room introducing me to Attorneys, Investigators, another Victim Advocate and the Division Chief who had initially rejected my case who happened to be sitting right next to me.

I took a deep breath, re-introduced myself and pulled out all of the binders of information that I had prepared for the meeting that day. I had learned over the years to become so detailed with my documentation of events that I was well prepared to answer just about every question that they threw at me.

I reviewed the case history and openly discussed my frustration with the system for not protecting my family and shared all of the mistakes and missteps by law enforcement and the prison system that had led us to this very moment. They listened, they were kind and they at least appeared to care.

At the end of the meeting they thanked me for my time and my courage and told me that I would be hearing something from their office notifying me of their decision within the next few days. I thanked them for their time and compassion and left the room feeling a sliver of hope which at this point was something that I was afraid to even feel anymore.

CHAPTER 44

The Phone Call

The next 72 or so hours are a blur. I did what I could to distract my mind from thinking about whether or not I had said or done the right things in the meeting with the team from the Attorney General's office. I was trying not to over analyze the meeting in my head or be upset at myself for leaving out a detail or forgetting a date.

On July 17, 2017, I received a phone call from an unknown Lansing number and I picked up the phone holding my breath. Somehow, I was able to say "Hello" and the voice on the other end introduced himself as Michigan Attorney General Bill Schuette. He went on to thank me for meeting with his team and commended me for my courage. AG Schuette then went on say the words that I had been waiting to hear for the past five years. "They were taking my case."

I'm not sure how long it took me to respond because I was equal parts happy, relieved and shocked to hear what he had just said. I of course thanked him and he let me know that his office would be putting out a press release that afternoon about them taking on my case. He added that someone from his team would be contacting me to talk further about next steps.

This was the best news that I had received in years and I honestly didn't even know how to feel anymore because I had been let down so many times in the past five years.

I sat in my room and let it all sink in for a few minutes as I processed the fact that I had just won a huge victory. My persistence, my refusal to stop telling my truth and the fact that I trusted my intuition had paid off. Going public and taking my story to the media as so many people had told me not to do was the best decision I had ever made.

Once I allowed myself to accept that the news that I had just received was real I allowed myself to feel some happiness, hopefulness and excitement, I immediately called Kristen Jordan Shamus at the Detroit Free Press, then my Mother, then Anna Slawson. This wasn't just my victory; this was our victory.

Press Release:

Schuette Charges Soon-To-Be Released Michigan Prisoner with Extortion, Witness Intimidation and Retaliation

Contact: Andrea Bitely, Megan Hawthorne; (517) 373-8060

July 18, 2017

LANSING – Michigan Attorney General Bill Schuette has today charged Kevin Beverly, 44, an incarcerated Michigan prisoner, with seven felonies related to alleged threats to his former wife, Nicole Beverly, and their two children.

"Living in fear is no way to live, and I won't stand by and let a victim continue to fear for her life and the lives of her children when I believe there is evidence of another crime having been committed," said Schuette. "Continued and targeted intimidation and retaliation is something that no one should have to experience."

The charges relate to a series of death threats made against Nicole Beverly. Evidence indicates that the threats were made in order to influence or control her testimony at a child support hearing, in retaliation for reporting his criminal activity and in retaliation for her victim impact statements delivered at a sentencing proceeding. Evidence indicates that threats against Nicole were made both directly to her, and to inmates housed at the same correctional facility.

The charges are as follows:

Jackson County:

1. Witness Retaliation, 4 counts, felony, 10 years

Beverly will be charged as a habitual offender, 2nd, increasing the maximum penalty to 15 years.

Affidavit

Washtenaw County:

2. Witness Intimidation, felony, 15 years

3. Extortion, felony, 20 years

Affidavit

Wayne County:

4. Retaliation for a Reporting a Crime, felony, 10 years

Kevin Beverly will be arraigned at all locations with the assistance of the Michigan Department of Corrections.

CHAPTER 45

Inside Evil with Chris Cuomo

By August of 2017 news about my case had grown even more viral and had hit news outlets across the country. I had many reporters reaching out to me for comment on my story and Channel 7 News in Detroit took a special interest in my case. They began following my story from start to finish alongside of the Detroit Free Press.

One day in August I received an email from an associate producer from the television series, Inside Evil with Chris Cuomo, that aired on HLN, a subsidiary of CNN. She was asking if I would be interested in sharing my story with a broader audience. I of course knew who Chris Cuomo was, but I had no idea that he had his own show. I was intrigued and agreed to a phone call to learn more.

When I spoke to the producers, they shared that they had been keeping an eye on my story for the past few weeks. They explained to me that the purpose of the show was to share true life stories of survival and human struggle and they felt that my story was one that could illustrate the fight that so many victims of domestic violence are up against when it comes to being believed and supported by the legal system.

They went on to explain that this would be a documentary style program and that they would be traveling here several times before and throughout the court trials to film and capture moments at court, at my home with my family as well as my personal feelings and emotions.

This was not what I had expected at all. I was expecting them to want me to do a onetime interview with Chris Cuomo and that would be it. Initially, I was feeling apprehensive because it sounded very overwhelming considering everything that I was already going through, and I didn't think it was something that I would be able to handle emotionally.

I asked them to give me two days to think about it and told them that I would get back with them. They agreed and said that they would understand my decision either way.

Over the next two days I did some serious soul searching and I talked to my most trusted friends about the opportunity that had just been presented to me. On one hand I knew that being on the show would be an incredibly challenging thing as it would force me to share my raw emotions with the world under the most difficult and vulnerable circumstances. On the other hand, I knew that this was an opportunity to share the realities and obstacles faced by domestic violence victims across our nation in real time, in a real-life situation and that others could see these harsh realities possibly for the first time in their lives.

In the end I decided that sharing the plight of victims of Domestic Violence and Stalking with the nation was bigger and more important than my vanity even if it meant I was ugly crying on national television and exposing my most vulnerable feelings and moments with the world.

In October of 2017, the HLN team flew out for the first of many filming sessions to follow. They were in the courtroom with me at most of the trial dates and were interviewing me before and after each event, capturing the intense emotions that I was experiencing throughout the entire ordeal.

Chris Cuomo flew out to Ypsilanti in December of 2017 to interview me and my family at our home. He was even brave enough to try some of my homemade moonshine. Chris was incredibly kind and considerate and is such a skilled interviewer that he absolutely touched on some of the deepest emotions that I was experiencing and had probably even hidden from myself.

They filmed so much footage over those eight months that I would joke that I finally knew what it felt like to be a Kardashian and I eventually quit apologizing when I would forget that I was wearing a microphone and would swear or say something inappropriate. In fact, they filmed so much footage that I had no idea how they could possibly take it all and turn it into an hour-long episode that was meaningful and would capture the most important parts of our story.

On July 9, 2018 they aired our episode of Inside Evil with Chris Cuomo for the first time. I was in awe of how well they were able to tell my story and share the plight of many domestic violence victims across the nation in such a respectful and meaningful way.

After watching the episode with two of my closest friends I knew that I had no regrets and was glad that I chosen to be vulnerable and put myself out there even when it was difficult in order to educate others who had never experienced domestic violence themselves. I also felt incredibly grateful that I was able to advocate for victims who may be going through something similar on a larger media platform.

CHAPTER 46

Wayne County

In October of 2017 the court dates began. Between October 2017 and May 2018, it truly felt like I was in court more than I wasn't. Since the Attorney General had charged my ex-husband for crimes in three separate counties it meant that we had pre-trials, follow up court dates and potential trials in all three counties.

On March 19, 2018 after multiple court dates my ex-husband plead guilty in Wayne County to Retaliation for Reporting a Crime. In return for his guilty pleas, Judge Ewell indicated that she was willing to reduce his sentence to 12 months in the Wayne County Jail, but only if he also agreed to plead guilty in a Washtenaw County trial court on the separate felony extortion charge he was facing there.

At first I was surprised by his decision to plead but then I realized that an additional 12 months in jail was nothing but a slap on the wrist for him and that he was probably feeling confident that Washtenaw County would offer him a very similar plea deal and he would be out of prison within the year with time served.

I remember interviewing with the HLN team outside of the courthouse that day telling them that I was having a hard time believing that he was going to plead guilty in both counties and I was not going to relax until everything was said and done. My gut was telling me that this felt way to easy and that was not my ex-husband's style at all.

CHAPTER 47

Washtenaw County

Our next court date was scheduled for the end of March in Washtenaw County. The expectation for court that day was that my ex-husband would be entering a guilty plea as he agreed to do with the Judge in Wayne County.

I remember waiting for what felt like a lifetime for them to bring my ex-husband and his attorney out from the room where inmates meet with council during hearings. His attorney Pete Tillman entered the room before him appearing frustrated and tense.

Once Kevin was settled at the table Judge Kelly asked them if they were ready to enter a plea. Kevin's attorney Pete stated exactly what I had been expecting to hear for the past two weeks. Kevin was not willing to plead guilty in Washtenaw County and was instead opting to go to full jury trial. His attorney then very dramatically slammed his brief case shut and walked out of the court room after requesting to withdraw from the case and being denied by Judge Kelly.

Judge Kelly set the Jury Trial to begin within the next week with the first day of jury selection being April 1st. My attorneys told me that while they were surprised, they were not shocked because if he had a chance to win a jury trial in any of the three counties it was in Washtenaw County as he was much more likely to have a liberal jury. I asked them what they thought the chances for conviction were considering that and they could only tell me that they would do the best that they could but there were no guarantees.

In many ways I was completely prepared for this to happen because my gut had told me that it would. It was still terrifying though to know that my fate and the fate of my children would now rest in the hands of the 13 strangers that would make up the jury.

CHAPTER 48

At the Mercy of Strangers

On April 1, 2018 jury selection began for the trial against my ex-husband. I was sequestered in the witness room with the investigators from my team who I had grown used to keeping me company during times like this. One of them was quiet and calm and the other had a very dark sense of humor similar to mine that kept me entertained and distracted when I needed it most. My victim advocates checked in with me when they could and by lunch time, they let me know that a jury had been selected and finalized.

For the rest of that first afternoon my friends and family stayed in the court room to hear the other witnesses that were being interviewed on the stand including the detectives that handled my case back in 2012, a forensic phone expert and my ex-husband's former Probation Officers. At the end of the day my attorneys came in to tell me that they had felt like everything had gone well so far and that I needed to be prepared to testify in the morning.

On April 2, 2018 I was set to be the first witness on the stand. My stomach felt like a ball of knots and I remember being so nervous that I was going to somehow screw up dates or times since everything had happened over such a long period of time. My victim advocate kept telling me that I would be fine and that I was one of the most reliable and believable witnesses he had ever seen in court.

The first thing that I noticed was that this court room was set up differently than most. The jury was off to my left side so I had to keep turning my body to make eye contact with them while I was speaking. I was seated directly in front of my abuser to testify. The best way that I can describe the way that I felt while I was on the stand was that time was moving in slow motion.

I had already trained myself that if I was asked to identify him by the clothing that he was wearing or that if for any reason I had to look towards him I would only look at him from the shoulders down or I would look straight through him, not at him. The way that this court room was set up made this very difficult.

It was very difficult because my attorneys had reminded me several times to keep turning to the left to make sure that the jury could hear me and that I was making eye contact with them while I was testifying. I remember asking my attorney for the documentation that I had kept during the time frame that my ex-husband was threatening and intimidating me for reference. I was so grateful that I had kept it since there is no way that I could possibly remember events from several years ago in chronological order.

I remember finishing my testimony and questions just before we were excused for lunch and I was put back into witness sequester. The attorneys and my victim advocate came in approximately two hours later to let me know that closing arguments were done and that the Judge was dismissing the jurors for the remainder of the day. In the morning they would begin deliberating their verdict.

That whole day is such a blur because of the emotional intensity that I was experiencing. I do remember how powerful it was for me to have so many of my survivor sisters and community members there in the courtroom as I was testifying. Many of them were wearing some version of the color purple which is the color that represents Domestic Violence Awareness. It gave me the strength and courage that I needed to keep going.

On April 3, 2018, we returned to the court house in hopes that the jury would reach a decision. It was such a surreal experience to sit there waiting with friends and loved ones for 13 strangers to decide my fate. There was nothing more that I could do or say at this point. I just had to hope and pray that we had done a good enough job to convince them to find him guilty of the charges.

At approximately 10 am my attorney let us know that the jury had requested to watch my recorded testimony again. I remember saying to him "okay, so that was like what 30 minutes that I was on the stand?" and him laughing and saying, "No, Nicole you were on the stand for over two hours." I was seriously shocked because I had absolutely no memory of being on the stand for that long. As a therapist I know that our brain's way of protecting us from traumatic situations is often by making them feel shorter, less intense or blocking memories entirely but I was still shocked to hear that I had been on the stand for that long. I asked him if it was good or bad that they were asking to watch my testimony again and him being very honest with me and saying, "I truly don't know Nicole. I could not get a read on them yesterday."

The jury broke for lunch and we all continued to hang out in the waiting area quietly filled with anticipation. The best comparison that I can give to what I was feeling was waiting at the hospital to get an update from the doctor about a loved one that had just undergone lifesaving surgery.

At approximately 3:00 pm we were told that the jury had reached a verdict and we were called back into the courtroom. I remember sitting on that hard-wooden bench, holding my breath waiting for the jury to re-enter the room and hand me my fate.

As the jury members re-entered the court room several of them made eye contact with me and I noticed that a lot of the jurors were coincidentally wearing purple that day which gave me even more hope.

I remember being very aware that the media cameras were focused on me as we all prepared to hear what the jury foreman was going to say. I put my head down, closed my eyes, held hands with the people on either side of me and braced for whatever may come next. And then she said the words, "We the jury find the defendant guilty.... on both counts of extortion and witness intimidation".

I burst into tears of joy... tears of happiness... tears of gratitude and tears of exhaustion. Before we left the courtroom, Judge Kelly let us know that sentencing would be held on May 15, 2018.

CHAPTER 49

Jackson County

Out of all the court dates aside from the jury trial in Washtenaw County the court dates in Jackson County were the most difficult for both myself and my family. They were the most difficult because that was where the other inmates testified to what my ex-husband planned to do to myself and my children once he was released from prison or if he was able to pay someone to do it for him.

All but one of the inmates agreed to testify and the one that refused to testify at the last minute made it obvious that he was concerned about retaliation if he did.

I was sequestered again during the testimony of the other inmates but when I saw my friends and family during the break, I could still see the tears and still feel the pain of having to sit and listen to what he was planning to do to us.

At some point during the day's testimony my ex-husband made the decision that pleading guilty to retaliation was in his best interest and I would not have to testify. At this point I was relieved because I was so emotionally and physically exhausted at that point that I just wanted this to be over with and my attorney's had told me that it would be very unlikely that he would get any more time added on even if he was found guilty by jury in Jackson County.

CHAPTER 50

Victim Statement

On May 15, 2018 we returned to court in Washtenaw County to hear the final sentence that would be issued by Judge Kelly now that a jury had convicted my ex-husband of both Witness Intimidation and Extortion. I finally had the opportunity to read my victim impact statement and I prayed that Judge Kelly would listen and would give my boys and I at least 5 more years of freedom but I was terrified.

When I was called up to speak, I took a deep breath and braced myself with one hand on the podium as I began to read my victim impact statement out loud.

Judge Kelly,

I am writing this letter regarding the sentencing of my ex-husband Kevin Beverly. Mr. Beverly was both physically and emotionally abusive towards me during our 18 years of dating and marriage. During the last year of our marriage the abuse became increasingly frequent and intense. Once during an incident of abuse where he hit, kicked and choked me, he held his gun to my head and told me all of the things he felt were wrong with me and all of the reasons that he should kill me. The next morning he made me apologize to him for "almost making him kill me".

I didn't leave or tell anyone about the abuse for some time because I was terrified of Mr. Beverly. He instilled fear in me by telling me almost daily that if I told anyone about his abuse or if I left him he would hunt me down like a dog and kill me and that no matter how

far I went or how hard I tried to hide from him he would find me. Mr. Beverly appeared to enjoy telling me all of the ways that he could and would hurt me if I left him. He would often tell me that he would take me by surprise and slit my throat, shoot me, torture me, disfigure me, paralyze me and that I would never live to see my children graduate from high school.

After I finally got up the courage to leave the marriage in 2009, Mr. Beverly's threats to kill me increased and he began to stalk me despite the personal protection order that was in place. As a result of his behavior between 2010 and 2011, I had to call the police 10 times due to his threatening and frightening behavior. In October of 2011 he was charged with aggravated stalking after stalking me outside of the police station where I was filing a report about his threatening to kill me yet again.

Once I left the police station he followed me and attempted to run me off of the road. He was arrested after police found him driving past my house later that night. That charge ended up being plead down to stalking and he was put back on probation after spending a few months in jail. Mr. Beverly then had a second aggravated stalking charge in 2012 related to more threats to kill me to which he plead guilty.

During the course of his incarceration for aggravated stalking the Michigan State Police have notified me that Mr. Beverly has solicited 4 separate individuals at 3 different correctional facilities to murder me and my children. I was also notified that 2 more individuals at Jackson Prison had come forward with written statements expressing that Mr. Beverly was repeatedly making statements in prison that as soon as he was released from prison he was going to come to my home and kill my children in front of me then torture me to death.

Through his words and actions over the past 7 years Mr. Beverly has repeatedly made it clear that he intends to kill me and my children upon his release from prison or will continue to attempt to hire others to kill myself and my children for him.

Unfortunately, because of Mr. Beverly's repeated threats to kill me and his attempts to solicit others to kill me I have become accustomed to living my life in fear and always looking over my shoulder. It is incredibly unfair to both myself and my two amazing children to have to live our lives this way.

We have become conditioned to always being aware of my surroundings, knowing where exits are, never sitting with my back to a door, triple checking locks and alarms, setting up passwords and lock down procedures at my work and my children's school and never being able to trust the intentions of unfamiliar people.

I have a great deal of difficulty sleeping at night and at times feel unsafe in my own home. Both my children and myself have attended counseling on and off over the past 7 years. I currently take medication prescribed by my doctor for anxiety and sleep.

As additional safety measures I have had to purchase a firearm, have a home alarm system installed and I have gotten a dog for protection. The Washtenaw County Sheriff's Department has red flagged our home as a priority for 911 calls, diagramed my home for SWAT team response and requested my family's dental records and fingerprints for identification purposes should something happen to us.

I have had to take many days off of work to meet with police and attorneys and attend various court proceedings. This has all definitely taken a toll on both my emotional and physical health over the years.

There are moments that I feel sorry for Mr. Beverly and the fact that he isn't able to be a part of our children's lives but then I remember all of the times that he has threatened to harm me and take that privilege away from me.

I am hopeful that in sentencing Mr. Beverly today you will take into consideration his pattern of abusive and threatening behavior and the level of risk faced by myself and my children and give us as many years as possible to live with less fear and anxiety.

Thank you for listening.

I took another deep breath and turned and went back to my seat. As we waited for Judge Kelly to speak and share her decision, I closed my eyes and braced myself for whatever she might say.

CHAPTER 51

Justice is Served

After what felt like a lifetime Judge Kelly began to speak and the entire court room became silent. She admonished Kevin for his behavior over the past few years and how he had intimidated me to the point that I had signed off on over $30,000 dollars in child support. She disregarded his plea to allow him to be released and enter into substance abuse treatment and he was ordered to serve consecutive sentences of five to 15 years in prison for witness intimidation, and eight to 20 years in prison for extortion.

This meant that he had just been sentenced to 13 to 35 years in prison with time served. He would next be eligible for parole in 2030. I felt like I could breathe again for the first time in weeks.

While it wasn't the life sentence that I had hoped for if he had been convicted of attempt to hire for murder, it was still a substantial sentence and I was incredibly grateful that I had at least 12 more years to live in peace before his next potential release date.

My friends, survivor sisters, family, victim advocates and the CNN crew all breathed a huge sigh of relief. After years of fighting I had finally won the most important battle of them all.

CHAPTER 52

The Road Ahead

It has been difficult at times to feel comfortable that my ex-husband will truly stay incarcerated until 2030 as he was sentenced to considering all of the times that I have been let down by the legal system. I have however, made a conscious decision not to live my life in fear because I believe that a life lived in fear is a life without joy.

People often ask me if I believe my ex-husband still wants to kill me or may again attempt to hire someone to kill me from prison and the short answer is Yes, absolutely. I do not believe he will have any magical transformation in prison that he has not had over the past 10 years since I left him. In fact it is much more likely that he will grow worse instead of better.

I know that I am going to have to relocate and change my name and social security number well before his release and my children and I will have to have conversations about whether or not it is in their best interest to do the same.

Because I know that my time being able to take a hard stance against Domestic Violence in the public eye is limited, I am making the absolute most of the time that I do have to advocate for change, help victims across the country and do prevention presentations at high schools and colleges. I try not to dwell on the negative and if I find myself feeling sorry for myself or my circumstances, I remind myself that I can only control certain things and dwelling on things outside of my control will only lead me to feelings of anger, frustration and sadness. Don't get me wrong, I definitely have days where I allow myself to feel all of these emotions, but I know now not to allow myself to get stuck there.

When I am doing speaking engagements and presentations people often ask me about dating and relationships since my divorce. It took me a long time to be ready to trust anyone or date again after my experiences with my ex-husband.

When I first started dating, I would run at any sign of something being off with someone, even if it was just in my own mind. As I healed emotionally, I identified "must have's" and "deal breakers" and created those lists to help me set boundaries for dating. If someone doesn't have my "must haves" or has to many "deal breakers" I know that a relationship with that person would not make me happy.

The few times I have bent my own rules, ignored red flags or read someone's personality traits through rose colored glasses I have regretted it and ended up either wasting precious time or walking away with a bruised heart. As a result, I have learned to keep my standards high and that I can be whole and happy on my own. The more we value ourselves and what we have to offer in a relationship the less likely we are to end up in a relationship that is toxic or abusive.

ACKNOWLEDGEMENTS

To my children, Myles and Carter, I never wanted this to be our family's story and I while I have many regrets, I am incredibly proud of both of you and the amazing young men that you have become. Please know that I would do anything to keep you safe and happy and that I love you both more than words can adequately express.

To my Mother and Father, Sally and Joseph Szilagyi thank you for raising me to be a strong and independent thinker, teaching me to use my voice and supporting me and my boys through both the best and worst of times.

To my sister, Christine Bernauer, thank you for helping us walk through the most dangerous of times.

To Prosecutor Arianne Slay, thank you for always being someone that I could turn to for help and for always showing up with tenacity, passion and dedication for my family and for all of the victims and families that you serve. I'll always have your 6!

To Prosecutor's Dan Grano and Robyn Lidell and John Lazet from the Attorney General's office, thank you for representing my family with passion, integrity and grace.

To all my victim advocates, Rochelle Wilson, Stacey Kearney, Christine Watson & Rebekah Snyder, thank you for keeping me informed, helping me stay sane, giving me hope and making me laugh even during the darkest of times.

To Deputy Paul Corrie from the Washtenaw County Sheriff's Department, thank you for taking the time to listen to my story and believe me. You were the first law enforcement officer that made me feel heard. We need many more officers like you in this world.

To Kristen Jordan Shamus, reporter at the Detroit Free Press, thank you for being the first to believe my story and share it with the world. Without your help and expert reporting skills my case would never had received the attention and outcome that it did. I am forever grateful.

To Dave Fair and WEMU, Thank you for always believing me, sharing my story and giving my voice a way to reach others that may need to hear it.

To Chris Cuomo and the HLN Family, thank you for expertly exposing the truths about the domestic violence epidemic while sharing our story with the world on our episode of Inside Evil with Chris Cuomo; Until Death Do Us Part.

To Cynthia Canti and State Side Radio; NPR thank you for taking an interest in my case and giving me opportunities to share my story and the plight of domestic violence victims across the nation.

To Simon Shaykhet and Channel 7 News in Detroit, thank you for taking an interest in my story and the plight of Domestic Violence Victims in the State of Michigan. Please continue to expose the injustices and struggles faced by victims until they are taken seriously with those with the power to make changes that will protect them.

To my Coworkers and Supervisors at Special Tree Rehabilitation and The WISD, thank you for your kindness, support, respect and understanding as I was navigating through some very difficult times. Your love, light and laughter helped me push through!

To my survivor sisters and brothers across the world, thank you for your love, kindness and support. Thank you for always keeping it real with me, checking me when needed and keeping me laughing. Your stories and experiences have given me hope and encouragement over the past 10 years and for that I am incredibly grateful for that.

To my "Heathens", Amy, Angie and Jenna, thank you for always helping me see through murky waters and get to shore when I most needed you!

To Barbara Niess-May and the Staff and Board Members of SafeHouse Center in Ann Arbor, MI thank you for inviting me to have a seat at the table to contribute to the work being done in our community!

To all of the other law enforcement officers, attorneys, judges and other helping professionals that have played a positive role in our story, thank you for all of the hard work that you do to help victims and survivors of intimate partner violence every single day!

To all of my friends, family members, former classmates and community members who have supported me on this journey, please know that your kindness, generosity and belief in me kept me going even on the darkest of days.

I wrote a large portion of this book at The Historic Lakeview Inn in Lakeview, Michigan. To the staff and owners there, thank you for the hospitality and peaceful and beautiful environment to write in. It wasn't until after I arrived at the Lakeview Inn that I learned that it has been a sought-after destination by many artists and writers over the years. I also learned upon arriving that the Inn's history includes the story that one of the previous owners had killed his second wife at the Inn and that she has reportedly been seen haunting the Inn by her husband, their gardener and several guests over the past 50 years.

BONUS GUIDE
SECTION INTRODUCTION

*This content is informational. It is not intended to serve as any psychological service/advice/diagnosis and is not a substitute for consultation with your health care provider. Not everyone is the same (e.g., abuse survivors, abusers, children, brain chemistry, etc) and different people may require different resources and supports than others.

While I was planning to escape my abusive marriage, I was desperate to find information about domestic violence. Information about how to safely leave my relationship, how to help my children cope, how this happened to me to begin with and how to heal from the trauma I had experienced.

I began to do research about domestic violence and safety planning while I was at work. I read articles about survivors who had made it out and found happiness again as well as countless articles about victims who were killed by their abusers after they left.

After I left my marriage, I continued to learn through my personal experiences both negative and positive as well as through the advice of my court advocates and the tribe of survivors that I connected with all over the world. I also continued to do research and read articles and books about safety, healing and the dynamics of abusive relationships so that I had a better understanding for myself and information that I could share with others.

Because I am a very vocal advocate and because my story has been shared on many different media platforms I am often contacted for advice by victims of domestic violence and stalking and their family members who need help. As a Clinical Social Worker who is also a survivor, I am also contacted by professionals who also have questions about working with victims and survivors of Domestic Violence and best practice for helping them through their recovery.

I have said for years that I was going to put together a "victim guidebook" where I could share the most meaningful and important information that I have learned and gathered over the years so that it could be accessible to more people.

The information that I am sharing in this section is my based on my personal experiences as both a Clinical Social Worker and Survivor and the research that I have done over the years. By no means am I saying that these are the only tools, tips and resources that will help victims of domestic violence and stalking.

I do however hope that you will find some of the information that I have learned along the way helpful and that it gives you some comfort to know that you are not alone on this journey.

BONUS GUIDEBOOK SECTION

Tips and Tools for Understanding the Many Layers of Domestic Violence, Safety Planning, Strategies for Surviving and Recovering from an Abusive Relationship

Part 1: Domestic Violence Does Not Discriminate... Knowing the Red Flags of Intimate Partner Violence.

Part 2: Understanding why Victims Stay.

Part 3: Understanding the common terms and forms of manipulation used by narcissists and those with abusive personalities.

Part 4: Safety Planning if you are still living with your abuser.

Part 5: Interacting with Law Enforcement

And documenting incidents of abuse and stalking.

Part 6: Home Security on a Budget

Part 7: Building resilience: Quick Tips for victims

Part 8: Strategies for victims, advocates, therapists, friends and family to help empower victims of abuse.

Part 9: Helping Children recover from living in an abusive household.

Part 1: Domestic Violence Does Not Discriminate . . . Knowing the Red Flags of Domestic Violence.

One of the main predictors for becoming a victim or perpetrator of domestic violence is growing up in a household where domestic violence has occurred and been modeled. That only makes sense because this would be an example of an intimate relationship that you grew up witnessing. It would feel normal and, in many ways, probably even comfortable for you to experience similar behaviors in your adult relationships.

I did not grow up in a household where domestic violence was occurring, but I also was never educated on the red flags of abuse or what to watch out for as a young adult in the dating world. I was naive and vulnerable at that time and I have always been an empathic person that liked to help others which made me the perfect target for my abuser.

It is important to know that most abusers are incredibly skilled at manipulation and deceit. Many people have told me over the years that they feel they "could never become a victim of domestic violence". Insinuating that they were too strong, too smart or too good to become a victim themselves.

I admit that had you told me as a young adult that my life would turn out the way that it did, I never would have believed you myself. I can however tell you with certainty that even the strongest, most intelligent and most beautiful of people can become the victim of a skilled abuser. I know this to be fact because some of the strongest, most attractive and most intelligent women that I know have become victims of domestic violence. Domestic Violence happens to people of all races, religions, genders, sexual orientations, education and income levels.

Abusive individuals are masters of manipulation. They slowly and strategically establish control and dependence of their victim through skilled manipulation, control and break down of the victim's self-esteem across all phases of the abuse cycle.

Abusers won't typically show their true selves in the beginning of a relationship because they are smart enough to know that we would know to take off our heels and run for the hills if they showed their true selves early on.

Obviously, no one is going to call you derogatory names or punch you in the face during your first few weeks of dating. Instead they will typically present as wonderful, loving, giving and almost perfect suitors.

These individuals will often attempt to rush you into a serious relationship, only wanting you to spend time with them, love bombing you with compliments, gifts and lifting you up onto a pedestal. They typically won't show you any of their outright negative or abusive traits until they are confident that they have you under their spell.

Looking back in hindsight victims will often say that they caught glimpses of their abuser's mask beginning to slip off even in the early stages of a relationship. Examples of this might be moments of anger and overreaction. For example, an overreaction to someone bumping into them while you are walking in a crowded area. The person expressing that they are feeling slighted in some way that does not make sense to you. The use of put downs or derogatory comments even if they are disguised as jokes or sarcasm and flashes of jealous or controlling behavior quickly explained away.

Common Red Flags

Intensity- An abusive individual will come on strong and may appear almost to be excessively charming in the beginning of a dating relationship. They will lie to cover up their past faults and insecurities. They will "love bomb" you with compliments, gifts and frequent texts and contact. The abuser will study you to see what your hopes, dreams and wants are and will quickly learn to play the part of your perfect match.

The abuser will try to win over your friends and family members by playing the perfect partner. Through their intensity they are sucking you into a relationship with them and making you fall in love with who they want you to believe they are before they let their mask of perfection begin to slip.

Many of the survivors that I know have shared with me that their relationships with their abusers were whirlwind romances that lead to quick marriages, moving in together quickly or having children together very quickly.

Jealousy- Responding irrationally to your interactions with other people. Becoming angry when you speak with the opposite sex and accusing you of flirting or cheating on them. Abusers will often attempt to make you believe that they are jealous only because they love you so much and can't imagine their lives without you. They will convince you that their expressions of jealousy are just expressions of love and concern.

Control- Telling you what you should or shouldn't wear either subtly through negative comments or outright. Telling you what you are allowed to do or who you can talk to or spend time with. Showing up uninvited at your home, school or work. Checking your phone for calls and texts, checking your social media sites for messages or comments on your posts. Checking your location to see if you are where you say you are throughout the day.

Isolation- Insisting that you only spend time with them. Giving you reasons why they don't like your friends, why they are bad for you and why you shouldn't spend time with them. Preventing you from spending time with your family. Through isolation they are increasing your emotional and psychological dependence on them.

Sabotage- They cause you to miss important events or cancel plans like parties, job interviews or family events by having a meltdown, getting sick, causing an argument or having some type of emergency just prior to the event happening. Hiding your phone, keys or other items of importance when you need them.

Criticism- Name calling, put downs and negative comments that are often disguised as jokes or sarcasm in the early stages of a relationship. Pointing out your faults and what they perceive as being wrong with you. Telling you that they are the only ones that care about you or could ever love you. Criticism will often be followed by apologies, gifts and empty promises. Through criticism they are strategically breaking you down and making you begin to lose self-confidence and question your own self-worth.

Blame- The abuser will begin to blame the victim for everything wrong in the relationship. Making you feel guilty for expressing your opinions or "making them angry". The abuser will often use gaslighting as a technique to make the victim believe that things did not actually happen the way that they remember or to convince them that they are crazy or dramatic and things really aren't "that bad" in the relationship.

Anger- Overreacting to small problems. Strong emotional reactions to daily stress or frustration. Throwing things, pounding walls or counters. Threatening others when upset. Coping with anger with the use of drugs and/ or alcohol. A history of violent or abusive behavior towards animals or other individuals. Any behaviors that make you feel uncomfortable or afraid should never be ignored. (Know the 8 Before it's Too Late, Beauty Cares.org)

History of abusive behavior- The likelihood that an abusive individual will admit to a history of abusive behavior is extremely low however many states have offender search lists, criminal history reports and public police reports at low or no cost. If someone tells you that the individual, you are dating has a history of abusive behavior it is important to investigate the matter seriously.

Abusers will often masterfully explain away someone else's accusations as them being "crazy, jealous, angry at them for a breakup or trying to get back at them for leaving a relationship".

Attempts to control your finances- An abusive individual may early on attempt to tell you what you should and should not spend money on. They may question your spending habits or request access to your financial information and accounts.

Part 2: Understanding why Victims Stay in Abusive Relationships

The most common reasons that victims stay too long in abusive relationships are love, fear, financial dependence, shame and lack of self-esteem, isolation and family pressure or expectations. There also is a physical, neuro-chemical component to why victims often feel driven to return to their abusers that is not talked about often enough by professionals.

- LOVE
- FEAR
- FINANCIAL
- SHAME/LACK OF SELF ESTEEM

- ISOLATION
- FAMILY
- NEURO-CHEMICAL

Love

- At some point, especially at the beginning of their relationship with their abuser was good, fun and loving… possibly for long periods of time. If the relationship was not positive at some point the victim would not have been drawn into it to begin with.

- Having experienced a positive and loving relationship with their abuser at some point in the relationship victims often have hope and truly believe their relationship can again be happy.

- Victims also often blame themselves for the demise of their relationships after being told that they are to blame by their abuser's countless times. Victims often believe if they try harder, stop upsetting their abuser or love them more their relationships can go back to loving and happy.

- Their abuser is also likely convincingly telling the victim that they love them, that they will change, they will get help, never hurt them again, go to counseling, stop drinking, stop using drugs, etc.…

The victim's abuser is also likely repeatedly telling them that no one else will ever love them as much as they do and that they will never find another person that will want to be with them.

Fear

The most dangerous time for a woman is when they leave their abuser because their abuser feels that they have lost their control and power. Here are a few reasons that fear can play such a powerful role in why victims stay.

- History of physical abuse and violence tells the victim that homicide is a real possibility.

- Their abuser likely threatens them in a very believable way that makes them for very good reason believe that if they leave, "they will kill them, hunt them down, kill their families, torture them", etc...

- Presence of a gun in the home increases risk of homicide by 500 times.

- The legal system often fails victims of domestic violence by not listening or taking them seriously when they ask for help.

- Weak sentencing guidelines and lack of understanding about domestic violence by family court workers, police officers, judges, etc… can put victims at risk of further harm by their abusers.

Financial Abuse

- Abusers often control the household finances and victims are not even aware of how much money is coming in and out of the household.

- Abusers often don't give victims access to checking accounts or credit cards but give them a small allowance instead.

- Abusers often convince their victims to quit working, stop schooling and "stay at home to take care of the household and children". Making them financially dependent on the abuser.

- Some abusers encourage the victim to live extravagantly, charge credit cards up and incur debt as a means of making it harder for them to leave.

- Shelters are often full and unable to take in victims.

- Victims often lack the skills and education level to obtain gainful employment.

Shame and Lack of Self-Esteem

- The abuser has over time convinced the victim that they are stupid, lazy, ugly, fat, crazy, worthless, unlovable and unable to survive on their own.

- The victim is terrified that they can't survive independently because that is the message they have been told repeatedly.

- The victim is embarrassed because society often tells that victims of domestic violence that they are somehow responsible for their abuse. That they stay so they must like it. That they somehow trigger or deserve to be abused.

- The victim is embarrassed if they haven't followed the advice of others and have gone back to the abuser.

- Poor response from law enforcement reinforces to victims that they are somehow responsible for their abuse.

- PTSD, depression, anxiety, lack of self-esteem, etc… also make it very difficult for victims to find and maintain gainful employment.

Isolation

- Across all phases of the abuse cycle the abuser attempts to isolate the victim from friends and family members so that their network of support begins to shrink, and the victim becomes more and more dependent on the abuser.

- The abuser will often complain about the victim's friends and family members and encourage the victim to stop spending time with them.

- The abuser will get upset, angry or sad when the victim does spend time with others and will often sulk, cry, rage or give the victim the silent treatment when the don't get their way.

- Over time the victim begins to find it easier to not deal with the abuser's reactions and will cut off relationships that they enjoy and find supportive.

- The abuser will often use excuses like "your family doesn't care about you", "your friends are a bad influence" or "none of them like me because they are just jealous of you.", to convince the victim that they are only looking out for the victim's best interest.

- Once the victim begins to cut off other relationships it leaves them feeling alone, isolated and much more vulnerable to the manipulative tactics being used by their abuser.

- Please leave the picture Carter's artwork as is per your question.

- There are two pictures that I would really like to add if possible. One under the chapter heading Growing Up Nicole and one at the top of the ENOUGH Initiative page. Please advise on how to do this if it is still possible.

Family

- The abuser threatens to take custody away from the victim.

- The abuser threatens to hurt or kill the children or family members of the victim.

- Society often tells victims that children need both parents in the home to be a real family.

- Society often tells victims that single mothers can't raise healthy boys without their father regardless of how unhealthy his behavior is.

- Some cultures and religions tell victims that they must stay married to their abusers despite being abused. This could put victims in further danger if they seek help or risk them being ostracized.

- Sometimes family members believe the gaslighting and manipulation of the abuser and further isolate the victim by taking the abusers' side.

Neuro-Chemical Component

- Recent studies show us that the neurobiological changes that take place for victims of abuse are likely very similar to those within the breakup phase of a non-abusive relationship. When any of us fall in love and connect with someone new, the neurochemistry of the reward system responds to establish this bond. In circumstances of abuse, the brain likely has the same attachment that anyone would have toward someone they love.

- Several important ingredients that contribute to someone's "addiction" to their abuser are oxytocin (bonding), endogenous opioids (pleasure, pain, withdrawal, dependence), corticotropin-releasing factor (withdrawal, stress), and dopamine (craving, seeking, wanting).

- Often when a person is traumatized by a romantic partner or someone they love, these chemicals become significantly dysregulated. With such strong neurochemistry in dysregulated states, it will be extremely difficult to manage emotions or make logical decisions.

- In the presence of such an addiction, there will often be intense craving, a heightened value attributed to the abuser, and a hyper focus on the relationship and conflict resolution. The victim's thoughts will often follow to make sense of these feelings. Her or his brain usually turns to self-deception and rationalizations of the abuser's behavior to resolve the cognitive dissonance (inconsistent thoughts). (Freeman, 2017)

- New research is showing us that up to 81% of victims of physical abuse by a partner have experienced at least one Traumatic Brain Injury (TBI).

- Very few victims are currently being screened for TBI by either health care professionals or domestic violence professionals.
- TBI can cause heightened anxiety, fear, memory loss, depression, mood swings, impulsive behavior, etc... depending on what part of the brain has been injured.

Part 3: Terms to familiarize yourself with that are related to Emotional Abuse and Narcissistic Personality Disorder which often go hand in hand or share very similar patterns.

Having a better understanding of common tactics used by abusive individuals and why they may have worked on us in the past can be incredibly empowering for victims of abuse. Once we are better able to understand the techniques and psychological warfare being used against us by abusive individuals the less likely we are to fall into their traps or be manipulated by them.

Terminology relating to narcissism and narcissistic personality disorder (NPD) has been developed by psychologists and therapists over decades of research as well as by survivors of narcissistic abuse seeking a vocabulary to understand and talk about their experience. This list is not meant to be exhaustive but rather an overview of some of the most useful terms for understanding the pathology of narcissism, emotional abuse and its impact on relationships and families. (J.Hall, 2017)

Denial

This is a compulsive feature of narcissism, whereby the narcissist willfully believes or pretends that traumatic events or circumstances do not exist or did not happen, even when presented with evidence to the contrary.

Devaluation

Because of their emotionally primitive perfect-or-worthless thinking (stuck at the developmental level of a young child) and their insistence on unattainable perfection, narcissists in relationships (with partners, family members, or friends) nearly inevitably become disillusioned. And because they lack a moral compass (again, like the stunted children they are), they do not hesitate to express their disappointment in a range of devaluing hostile behaviors, including judgment, belittlement, and rage, if not outright abandonment.

Divide and Conquer

This is a primary strategy narcissists use to assert control, particularly within their family, to create divisions among individuals. This weakens and isolates family members, making it easier for the narcissist to manipulate and dominate. The narcissist sets up an environment of competition and terror in which individuals are trying to avoid attack, often at one another's expense. S/he favors some and scapegoats others, breeding mistrust and resentment among siblings or between the other parent and children. Such dynamics also can play out in a work setting, where a boss uses the same kinds of tactics to control and manipulate employees.

Enabler

Usually a partner/spouse of the narcissist, enablers "normalize" and even perpetuate the narcissist's grandiose persona, extreme sense of entitlement, and haughty attitude and behavior toward others by absorbing the abuse and acting as an apologist for it. Enablers are always avoiding conflict and attack while often also seeking rewards such as affection, praise, power, gifts, or money. Enablers may be under the delusion that they are the only ones who can truly understand the narcissist and oftentimes sacrifice or scapegoat their children to placate the narcissist.

Flying Monkeys

Like the flying monkeys who served the Wicked Witch of the West in *The Wizard of Oz*, flying monkeys in the narcissistic family are enablers who help with the narcissist's dirty work, often to avoid being targeted themselves and/or to benefit from a certain level of bestowed privilege. The most manipulable types make the best flying monkeys. They may be children or other relatives.

Gaslighting

This is a form of psychological abuse in which narcissists systematically undermine other people's mental state by leading them to question their perceptions of reality. Narcissists use lies and false information to erode their victims' belief in their own judgment and, ultimately, their sanity. Common gaslighting techniques come in the form of denying and projecting: After an abusive incident, narcissists refuse responsibility, blame the abused, or outright deny that the abuse took place. They may say things like, "You're too sensitive," "You're crazy," "That's not what happened," "Why can't you let anything go," or "You made me do it." The term *gaslighting* comes from the 1944 Hollywood film *Gaslight,* a classic depiction of this kind of brainwashing.

Gray Rock

Going "gray rock" is a boundary-setting and conflict-avoidance strategy that can be effective in dealing with narcissists. It simply means making yourself dull and nonreactive, like a colorless unmoving rock. In gray-rock mode, you engage minimally with the narcissist and his/her circus of enablers/flying monkeys. You do not show or share your thoughts or feelings. You do not react to antagonism and manipulation. In short, you make yourself of little interest to the narcissist.

Hoovering

Since narcissists are by nature pathologically self-centered and often stunningly cruel, they ultimately make those around them unhappy, if not miserable, and eventually drive many people away. If people pull away or try to go no contact, narcissists may attempt to hoover (as in vacuum suck) them back within their realm of control. They try to hoover through a variety of means, from promising to reform their behavior, to acting unusually solicitous, to dangling carrots such as gifts or money. However, if they find replacement sources of supply they may simply walk away from old ones.

Narcissistic Rage

Narcissistic personalities often react with rage when their underlying feelings of vulnerability and shame are triggered. They tend to take even small slights, which most people would easily brush off, as intensely humiliating. When this happens, their fabricated "perfect" self and overblown feelings of entitlement are threatened, setting off a wild rage response. Narcissistic rage is terrifying, sometimes physically violent, and far beyond normal anger. It is emotionally and physically traumatizing for those on the receiving end, particularly children, who naturally blame themselves for adults' reactions.

Narcissistic Supply

People with narcissistic personality disorder depend emotionally on others to sustain their sense of identity and regulate their self-esteem. They get their narcissistic supply either by idealizing and emulating others or by devaluing and asserting their superiority over others. Anyone they can manipulate—a partner, child, friend, or colleague—is a potential source of supply. Without suppliers, narcissists are empty husks. If a source of supply pulls away, they may attempt to hoover them back and/or look for other sources.

No Contact

People who have been abused by a narcissist may choose to cut ties altogether with that person. Typically, people who end up going no contact have had their boundaries violated in traumatic ways that eventually push them to shut down all communication with the narcissist. For adult children of narcissists, going no contact is typically a deeply ambivalent and painful choice that feels like a matter of survival in order to break the cycle of hurt and to attempt to heal. Going no contact, especially from a parent, is difficult to explain to people who don't understand narcissism and its devastating effects, further isolating victims.

Smear Campaign

Narcissists engage in smear campaigns to discredit others within their family or social sphere. Narcissists may smear another person because that person sees through their mask, they are trying to conceal preemptively their own abuse of that person, or they are taking revenge because the person offended or rejected them. Narcissists may conduct a smear campaign for lesser reasons, such as jealousy or resentment. Narcissists can be quite calculating in their process of discrediting and socially isolating their target, using innuendo, gossip, and outright lies to family, friends, neighbors, and community members. Narcissists won't hesitate to smear an ex to their children, a scapegoated child to friends and relatives, or a colleague to other colleagues. The smear campaign usually happens behind the victim's back, often with the assistance of the narcissist's enablers/flying monkeys.

Part 4: Safety Planning. Tips if you are still living with your abuser or being actively stalked by your abuser

- Try to keep your phone charged and near you at all times in case you need to use it for an emergency.

- Keep an extra set of keys hidden somewhere that are easily accessible either inside or outside of your home should you need to leave, and your abuser has taken your keys from you as they typically will when they begin to escalate.

- Identify the safest room in your house in case you need to isolate yourself or yourself and your children from your abuser. Try to pick a room with a locking door and a door or window to the outside should you need to escape from it. It would be best to keep your emergency bag and documents hidden in this room if possible.

- Mentally or physically practice getting to this room and securing it as quickly as possible should an emergency arise.

- Set up a code word or phrase with a trusted family member or friend so that should you need for them to call 911 on your behalf they will know what to do. Try to pick a code that is somewhat of a common phrase that abuser will not pick up on it should they overhear the conversation. Ex: 'The weather has been really crazy today" or "

- Also set up a code word or phrase with children that are old enough to understand so that they know when to quickly head to the "safest room" you have identified or to call 911 for help.

- Set up a designated meeting space for you to meet up with your children should you become separated during violence or escape from the home. (Example: a neighbor's house, park or nearby store.

- If violence becomes unavoidable make yourself as small of a target as possible by curling up into a ball and protecting your face and head by putting your arms and hands around each side of your head fingers entwined.

- Don't wear scarves or long necklaces that your abuser could use to strangle you with.

- If possible, keep an emergency bag with some clothes, needed medication, cash, gift cards and any other personal items that have deep meaning to you. If possible, keep this bag hidden in your "Safest Room".

- Keep documents of copies of important documents in your emergency bag as well. Birth certificates, social security cards, bank account and insurance information as well as marriage license, important phone numbers and addresses should you need to make a quick escape.

- Make a habit of backing your car into your garage or driveway for quick escape.

- If there are weapons in the house, try to make sure that they are locked away if possible and report the to the police immediately if you need to call 911.

- Try to create a peaceful space for yourself where you can read, draw, paint, complete hobbies or meditate.

- Rehearse your safety plan in your head so that you feel more confident about staying safe.

- Identify three positive things in your life every day and remind yourself of them when you are feeling low.

- Try and establish a self-care routine with exercise, yoga, walks, meditation, regular bedtime and wake time.

- Trust your gut. If you feel like you are in danger call 911 and lock yourself into your safest room until help arrives.

- This is a very difficult time, but it is important to remember that there is help and there are resources available when you are ready to leave your abusive relationship. There will never be a perfect time to leave but once you find yourself ready you will find there is a large network of agencies and survivors to support you through the process...

Part 5: Interacting with Law Enforcement And documenting incidents of abuse and stalking.

As a victim of Domestic Violence and/or Stalking the likelihood that you are going to have to interact with law enforcement officers and court officials is high. As a result, I highly recommend that victims always keep a dedicated notebook with them to document any type of abusive behavior, stalking behavior, calls to law enforcement and their responses.

When we are experiencing trauma, our brains do their best to protect us. As a result, we may not remember details like times, dates, names of officers or witnesses and our abusers attorney's love to use that against us an opportunity to look like unreliable witnesses or accuse us of lying or making things up.

I learned quickly that without keeping notes for myself so much information was lost from my memory by the next day I began to carry my notebook with me everywhere I went and did my best to follow a simple format.

In the beginning I would then input the information into a file that I kept on my computer once I was home safely and calm enough to do so. I did this so I would have a backup should anything ever happen to my notebook and to make it easier to email the information to people as needed.

During my court hearings my documentation ended up being crucial as I never would have remembered the details of events from years earlier.

Sample Format for documentation

- Date:
- Time:
- What happened:
- Were there witnesses/names and contact information if possible.
- Did you call the police?
- If yes, what officer responded and what did they say:
- Ask for the officer's card and police report number.
- Take pictures or video if possible, of any marks, bruises or property damage.
- This same format applies to phone conversations with your abuser, law enforcement officers and court officials.

Example:

Date: September 2, 2020

Time: 11:00 pm

Event: At approximately 11:00 pm I heard someone turning my front, then side door knob. I then heard the trees rustling along the side of my home. My dog began barking.

Witness: My son was home with me and heard the noises as well.

Action: I called 911 at 11:04 pm

Police response: Officer Bryant responded at 11:28 pm.

Result: Officer Bryant took the information and walked around my home with a flashlight but did not find anyone outside. He gave me his card and report #98346.

Other: No pictures or video, unable to sleep all night for fear that my ex-husband would try and enter our home during the night.

Part 6: Home Security on a Budget

When I first left my ex-husband, I had no extra money in the budget for security measures like an alarm system or security cameras. I know that in the past few years many new less expensive systems have been introduced that appear to be reliable. I would recommend researching cost and/or asking alarm companies if they offer discounts for domestic violence and stalking victims.

Because I did not have the means to afford an alarm system at that time, I went to the hardware store and purchased very inexpensive two dollar door and window alarms that activated if anyone attempted to open the door or window they were placed on. I also purchased a few "door jammers" that you place on the inside of doors that make it more difficult for someone to push their way in.

Before I purchased and trained with my firearm I kept pepper spray and a self-defense tool on my key chain as well as pepper spray and hornet spray on my bedside table and kitchen counters in case my abuser got into my home and I need to defend myself.

I also purchased solar powered spotlights for five dollars apiece at my local family dollar. These inexpensive lights did the tJames at lighting up dark corners and entryways.

Two of the most vulnerable entry points of a home are the sliding glass door and windows. This is because the locking mechanism on these types of barriers is really nothing more than an aluminum latch that can be easily defeated.

Many sliding glass doors can be easily pried open at the latch. Therefore, it's important to have a security mechanism in place that prevents the door from being slid open once unlocked. This can be as easy as placing a solid wooden rod or dowel (such as a closet rod) or a piece of rebar steel cut to size in the track of the door. Most home improvement stores will cut these materials to size for you at no additional cost. All you need to do is provide the measurements.

A simple way to prevent a sliding door from being lifted out of its tracks is to install a few large sheet-metal or wood screws into the upper track of the door. Each screw should be placed a few inches apart and screwed in just deep enough to where the top of the door barely touches the heads of the screws when it slides back and forth.

To prevent windows that slide vertically from being opened, install a large screw a few inches above the top of the window on both sides of the frame. This will allow you to open the window to enjoy fresh air when needed yet prevent the window from being opened any wider than a few inches.

I had my two recessed basement windows replaced with glass blocks so that they could not be an entry point for my abuser. I also had reinforced pieces of plywood painted to match my door and trim and screwed into the wood frame that that held my sidelight windows in. The plywood would at least slow him down if he was trying to break through the glass to reach in and unlock my door.

For your safety and the safety of your family, however, make sure you have a hammer or similar tool to shatter the glass in case a window is needed as an escape route during a fire or other emergency.

Another effective yet inexpensive way to deter intruders is to add a few psychological deterrents around your home. Here are a few more low-cost ideas.

Install "Dummy Security Cameras" outside of your home. Security cameras can be quite effective in deterring individuals attempting to enter your home. However, if you can't afford the real thing, there are inexpensive dummy cameras on the market that work well as a deterrent by those who believe they are real.

Explore the possibility of adopting a dog. In addition to making great companions, dogs are naturally loyal and protective of their owners and home. The moment a dog sees or hears something out of the ordinary, it will often bark out of instinct to alert its owner and warn the offender.

If you don't have the means to care for a dog, sometimes all it takes is to create the appearance that you own one to deter individuals. This can be easily accomplished by purchasing and displaying "Beware of Dog" signs around the outside of your home. Purchasing signs with the name or picture of a large, protective dog breed such as a Rottweiler, German Shepherd, or Doberman Pincher can also add to the psychological effect of the signs.

Place security alarm signs and decals on the outside of your home. Just as Beware of Dog signs can deter people, so can displaying home security alarm signs and decals around your property. In addition to displaying signs outside the exterior of your home, place a security alarm decal near the latch on the interior of each of your at-risk windows and sliding glass doors.

To someone that has not experienced stalking or being constantly threatened and harassed by an abusive individual this may all sound extreme and over the top... for someone living their life constantly looking over their shoulder and afraid to close their eyes to sleep at night this is just a small bit of peace of mind.

Part 7: Building resilience: Quick Tips for victims to catch their footing

- Participate in individual and/or group therapy as soon as possible after leaving your abusive relationship. Many shelters, colleges and women's centers offer free counseling.

- Allow yourself to forgive yourself. (Staying, believing, hoping, past choices, etc…) This may have to start in baby steps but if we hold onto guilt and shame for too long we cannot move forward in the healing process.

- Understand that you will never get the apology or answers you want from your abuser and that is okay. Create your own closure.

- Spend time with friends and doing things you enjoy even if you are doing it by yourself.

- Take time off from dating until you are 100% okay with being alone. You need to heal.

- Tell your story… verbally, through writing or artwork.

- Exercise, even if it is just taking a 15 minute walk a few times a week. Exercise is great for stress reduction and boosts that positive brain chemistry.

- Do you best to eat healthy foods, get enough sleep and drink lots of water.

- Take a self-defense class.

- Get a dog or alarm for home security.

- Set goals for yourself and create a plan.

- Create a vision board that reflects your goals and hang it somewhere that you will see it often to reinforce what you are working towards.

- Give yourself permission to grieve and experience all of your emotions. The end of a relationship no matter how bad it was is still a loss that we experience, and it is normal to grieve it's ending.

- Write on your mirror messages of self-love and make yourself say them out loud every day.

- Make an "I can do this box" that every day you write something positive that you did or that happened to you. Read the notes whenever you are feeling down.

- Whenever you start to feel overwhelmed or panicked imagine a stop sign, take 5 deep breaths then picture a safe place or happy thing and tell yourself positive things like "you can do this, you are okay, you are a survivor" until you feel back in control. (Early on I wore a rubber band on my wrist that I would snap when I found myself having difficulty and becoming stuck in a negative mindset).

- Don't fixate on the negative and what could have been… stay forward focused on the positive and what is going to be.

- Stay away from negative people or people who make you feel bad about yourself. It is okay to say "No" and set healthy boundaries for yourself.

- Unless it is court ordered related to custody do not have any contact with your abuser… any contact that you have opens the door for them to have some power over you or come back into your life.

- Establish or re-establish a relationship with God or another higher power or explore different spiritual practices to see if there are any that give you comfort and peace.

- Create a playlist of music that is uplifting and makes you feel strong and happy. Listen to it whenever you start to feel down.

- Connect with other survivors either in person or online. They can become your lifeline and support system.

- Join a support group through a local domestic violence agency.

- Follow domestic support pages and groups on Facebook and Instagram such as; The ENOUGH Initiative, Jenna's Journey, Butterflies Free of Domestic Violence, Life After Domestic Violence, etc...

- Meet up and spend time informally with other survivors of Domestic Violence.

- If you decide to get a firearm for protection make sure that you go through the proper training and obtain your license to carry a hand-gun so that you can safely protect yourself and not get into trouble with law enforcement yourself.

- When you are ready, advocate and share your story to others. By telling our stories, we give others hope that they can also overcome their abusive relationship. You may also find that becoming an advocate can be very rewarding and can help you along your healing journey as you help others heal as well.

Part 8: Strategies for victims, advocates, therapists, friends and family to help empower victims of abuse.

From my personal experience as a survivor of domestic violence and the experiences of countless other victims that I have interviewed and met with over the past six years I have learned that in order to help victims, become and remain survivors of domestic violence it is important for us to focus on combating the reasons that victims typically stay in abusive relationships and help support them in breaking through each of those barriers… Some of those reasons again are Love, Fear, Financial Abuse, Isolation, Shame, Family and Brain Chemistry Changes.

As therapists and advocates we can't enforce this, but it is highly recommended that victims do not begin to date after leaving an abusive relationship for at least a year. They need an emotional de-toxification from their abusive relationship and time to heal.

During that first year they need to find themselves again, understand what happened to them and why, establish healthy boundaries and learn the red flags so they can recognize them easily.

Individuals who rush into new relationships very often end up dating another abusive individual. Often survivors will involve themselves with someone "less abusive" than their previous abuser and justify that this person is "better than" than their abuser. For example, they will accept emotional abuse because it is better than physical abuse or controlling behavior because they aren't being hit.

Encourage the victim to have no contact with their abuser unless there is a court order forcing them to have contact related to child custody. Contact allows the abuser to continue to manipulate, abuse and have power over the victim. It also gives them an opportunity to convince the victim to allow them back into their life and begin the cycle again.

After leaving their abuser victims often have no idea who they truly are anymore because their abuser has been the one telling them how to act, how to dress, what to eat, what to do, etc… The victim needs to explore their wants, needs and likes to determine what their interests are explore what they enjoy. Encourage them to try new things and explore their community.

Tips to Combat Low Self Esteem and Loss of Self Identity as the victim's relationship has come to an end. (Love of self)

- Encourage the victim to practice positive self-talk daily.

- Encourage the victim to journal their stories and emotions.

- When appropriate encourage the victim to write a letter that will later be destroyed expressing to their abuser exactly how they feel without restraint. The letter should then be ripped up and disposed of or burned as a form of closure.

- Encourage the victim to exercise, eat healthy foods and drink lots of water. The healthier we feel physically has a direct impact on our emotional well-being.

- Encourage the victim to start exploring new hobbies and activities.

- Help the victim replace their abuser's negative words with words of self-love and empowerment by creating transformation picture collages using pictures of them during abuse with negative associations and pictures of them free of their abuser and healing.

Tips for Helping Victims Combat Fear

- Help the victim create a safety plan and remind them to practice it regularly.

- Help the victim obtain a personal protection (PPO) order or no trespassing order if PPO is denied.

- Encourage the victim to call the police every time the PPO is violated, or their abuser does something threatening or violent if they do not yet have a granted personal protection order.

- Help the victim find resources for a house alarm or window alarms, self-defense classes, dog adoption, childcare, etc…
- Encourage the victim to document all attempts and forms of contact from their abuser.
- Trust that the victim's fears are legitimate.

Tips for Combating Financial Abuse

- Connect the victim with local domestic violence agencies and resources. Staying in a shelter is often the last desired resort for most victims but shelters are often the fastest way to gain resources for housing, financial and employment assistance programs as well as help with legal issues.
- Assist the victim in applying for cash assistance, food stamps, Medicaid, childcare, housing assistance, etc… as soon as possible.
- Connect the victim with job placement agencies, career counseling and/or college or technical training opportunities.
- Connect the victim with local food pantries, churches and clothing closets for resources.
- Encourage the victim to ask for help from family and friends in case of emergency.
- Go Fund Me accounts are another popular resource for victims to utilize for emergency funds if they are comfortable sharing their needs publicly.
- Connect the victim with free credit recovery and financial literacy programs.
- It is important to remember that if a victim does not have the financial means to support themselves, they are much more likely to return to their abuser out of necessity.

Tips to Combat Isolation

- Encourage the victim to begin individual therapy if that is not your role with them.

- Encourage the victim to join a domestic violence support group.

- Encourage the victim to join another group or activity where they can meet new people. Ex: Church, book club, single parents' group, walking group, etc...

- Encourage the victim to spend time with friends and family.

- Encourage the victim to connect with other victims, survivors and support networks online.

- Help the victim create a list of things that they can do when the begin to feel lonely and are tempted to reach out to their abuser or engage in another unhealthy behavior. Ex: Call Renee, Take a walk, Listen to music, Watch a movie, sleep, etc...

- Help them find these organizations and online communities as they may be too overwhelmed in the beginning to do it on their own.

- Tips to Combat Feelings of Shame

- Educate the victim or encourage the victim to educate themselves about the tactics of abusers, gaslighting and manipulation. This knowledge will help them understand that they are not to blame for what happened to them. Help them find books, websites, Facebook pages and articles that will provide them with information and insight.

- Encourage the victim to read books and articles written by survivors that can be motivational and inspiring.

- Connect the victim with other survivors that have are involved in advocacy work and can help them understand that they are not to blame.

- Encourage them to own their story and what happened to them. Tell their story to others… Ownership of our stories is a very powerful thing.

Tips to Combat Obstacles Around Family

- Remind the victim that staying with their abuser was not healthy for their children. Let them know that growing up witnessing an abusive relationship greatly increases the chances that those children will repeat the abuse cycle as an abuser or victim.

- Help the victim establish healthy boundaries with family members.

- Conduct family therapy sessions (Not with the abuser) if appropriate.

- Recommend individual or group therapy for other family members if appropriate.

- Provide domestic violence education/information to family members to help them understand the cycle of abuse, the reasons victims often stay and how to best support their loved one.

Tips to Combat Neuro-Chemical Changes

- Provide the victim with information about the neuro-chemical changes the brain experiences when in an abusive relationship. There are many books and articles that share research that has been done on the topic. Sometimes a victim understanding that there can be a physical component causing them to react in certain ways can be extremely empowering.

- Encouraging victims to maintain the 'no-contact' approach is often helpful. If there is no contact the brain does not have the chance to automatically release attachment chemistry in response to the partner, particularly if he is demonstrating good behavior.

- One of many ways' victims can help their brain break a trauma bond is by facilitating the release of calming oxytocin (from the amygdala). Igniting oxytocin receptors of this type can reduce cravings, ease withdrawal, and lessen pain. (Freeman, 2017)

- Encourage the victim to explore other means of releasing oxytocin such as increasing opportunities for positive social interactions with others, soaking in a hot tub, petting a dog, trying yoga and meditation. Other means of increasing oxytocin are physical contact with others such as hugs and massages and by expressing gratitude and doing kind things for others.

- If appropriate have the victim evaluated for a potential Traumatic Brain Injury or Chronic Traumatic Encephalopathy for more severe symptoms. It is estimated that 81% of victims of domestic violence have sustained at least on brain injury related to physical abuse.

Part 9: Helping Youth who have Experienced Domestic Violence

Introduction by Nicole Beverly, LMSW

Statistics tell us that children who have grown up in a household where Domestic Violence is occurring are at much greater risk of becoming either the victims or perpetrators of domestic violence in the future. As a parent of children who have witnessed Domestic Violence it is only normal for us to worry about our own children after we have left our abusive relationships.

Children who have witnessed and experienced Domestic Violence occurring in the home may develop symptoms of Post-Traumatic Stress such as anxiety, depression, not eating, not sleeping, experiencing nightmares, mood swings, etc...

It is important to give children healthy outlets for their feelings as soon as possible and allowing them to express their emotions without judgement through individual or group counseling. Focusing on development of positive coping and self-regulation strategies is equally important as it is likely that negative strategies have been modeled for them in their households and may have already become learned behaviors.

Written by Lindsey Birrell, LMSW candidate, Wayne State University

The unseen victim of domestic violence is the child of the victim/abuser. Children who are present during abuse of any type, regardless of age, experience trauma. Having a connection with both the victim as well as the abuser can make the abuse extremely difficult to comprehend and understand. Because of this, many children who have grown up in households witnessing domestic violence have shown higher rates of mental illness and social difficulties as they age.

- Data shows children who have been exposed to DV at home have significantly higher levels of psychopathological indicators and more issues with relationships with others, (Diez, Alonso, Ezama & Gomez, 2018).

- Support groups as well as individual therapy for children who have witnessed DV are shown to be successful, (Mullender, 2004). Though rates are shown to be higher, there are ways to minimize the risk and to reduce the impact on the child.

- Trauma care focuses on addressing the abuse as a trauma in the child's life and working with the child to cope properly with that trauma. Allowing a child to feel as if they are not alone or at fault in the situation through support groups involving other children who have also witnessed domestic violence at home is shown to be incredibly helpful to the developing mind.

  - Immediate trauma care is shown to be beneficial in helping to reduce symptoms of PTSD in children who have experienced DV during childhood, (Paul, 2019).

  - School-based support groups have been shown to be effective in building relationship and providing a positive space for healing, (Beetham, Gabriael & Hazel, 2019).

- Education for youth can help prevent the continuation of the cycle. Many youth who grow up in homes with domestic violence end up continuing the cycle within their own relationships be it becoming a victim or even an abuser. Through education of the red flags and ways to prevent DV, the cycle can be broken.

- In trainings done with The ENOUGH Initiative, data shows 60% of the youth in attendance know of someone who has been in an abusive relationship. The same data shows that the presentations are shown to provide an increase in knowledge of red flags of DV, reasons people stay in abusive relationships and ways to help (Birrell, Beverly & Wells, 2020).

Beetham, T., Gabriel, L., & Hazel, J. (2019). Young Children's narrations of relational recovery: A school-based group for children who have experienced domestic violence. Journal of Family Violence, 34 (6), 565-575. Birrell, L., Beverly, N. & Wells, K. (2020). The ENOUGH Initiative: An evaluation of adolescent learning of DV/IPV prevention.

Díez, C., Fontanil, Y., Alonso, Y., Ezama, E., & Gómez, L. E. (2018). Adolescents at serious psychosocial risk: What is the role of additional exposure to violence in the home? Journal of Interpersonal Violence, 33 (6), 865–888.

Freeman, R. (2017). The Brain Can Work Against Abuse Victims. Psychology Today, January 18, 2017

Hall, J. (2017). Narcissism 101: A Glossary of Terms for Understanding the Madness. Narcissistic Family Files, September 19, 2017

Mullender, A. (2004). Tackling domestic violence: providing support for children who have witnessed domestic violence.

POEM

Finding Nicole 2013

I long to be her again... to be ordinary, normal, happy, me...

I long to be a woman that only has to worry about things like what she's making for dinner or how she should cut her hair...

Where she wants to travel or what color to paint her bedroom walls...

But I know that he lurks, stewing in anger and hatred just waiting for his chance.

Plotting, planning and craving to end what is left of me.

I must prepare, plan, strategize... Strengthen my body and mind.

Always looking over my shoulder, prepared for anything and ready to fight for my life.

If I'm honest I sometimes find myself looking for danger, testing my nerve and strength...

A walk at night, leaving a bar alone at 2 am, a stranger too quick to become a friend.

I have built my walls high, too high.... I've built them with mortar and steel sprinkled with gold dust.

No one is every truly invited inside of these gold dust covered walls...

I draw them near only to push them away.

It's just easier that way, no bonds, no disappointments, no hurt...

I've been told that I'm too strong, too alpha, a lone wolf... that I have an icy heart...

Perhaps that's true but I did not choose to become this...

This, this thing that I have become...

This thing created by pain, anger, sadness, rage and fear...Fear that never sleeps, it even visits me in my dreams.

No rest for the weary...

Fear serves to remind me that he's out there somewhere lurking, plotting, craving to have his chance to end what's left of me...

I long to be her again, that girl I used to be...

Ordinary, normal, happy, free... Me.

—Nicole Beverly

Information about the Author Nicole Beverly, LMSW and Founder of The ENOUGH Initiative.

Nicole Beverly is a Clinical Social Worker and the Founder and President of The ENOUGH Initiative based in Ypsilanti, MI.

The ENOUGH Initiative is a Non-profit 501c3, Domestic Violence Prevention Organization. It is the mission of The ENOUGH Initiative to provide education and information to young adults aged 14-24 about the red flags of domestic violence and how to respond if you see it happening in your community as well as victim education, empowerment and resilience building.

Information about The ENOUGH Initiative:

Website: www.the-enoughinitiative.com

Facebook: The ENOUGH Initiative

IG: enoughinitiative

Twitter: @enough-dv

Email: theenoughinitiativedv@gmail.com

Nicole Beverly, LMSW also does public speaking engagements and events to help educate groups, businesses and communities about Domestic Violence, Prevention and ways to end victim stigmatization.

More information about Nicole Beverly:

Facebook: Nicole Beverly;DV Survivor, Speaker & "Finding Nicole" Book page.

Website: findingnicole.vistaprintdigital.com

Email: Findingnicole19@gmail.com

Youtube: Nicole Beverly

The National Domestic Violence Hotline:

1-800-799-7233

www.thehotline.org